LEADERSHIP PARADOXES

Leadership remains one of the most sought-after qualities in contemporary society, yet after centuries of research, education and debate it remains just as elusive as ever. *Leadership Paradoxes: Rethinking Leadership for an Uncertain World* argues that the key to understanding and enhancing leadership education, theory and practice lies in the recognition of its paradoxical tendencies.

Through in-depth analysis of seven interconnected paradoxes the international team of contributors illustrate the tensions, dilemmas and challenges faced by leaders and managers in organisations, and suggest ways in which they can be reconceived as opportunities to be embraced rather than as problems to be solved. This book is supported with reflective and discussion questions for each chapter as well as a companion website at leadershipparadoxes.com which offers further material and also a channel for discussion.

Leadership Paradoxes will be valuable supplementary reading for students of leadership at advanced undergraduate, postgraduate, and post-experience level.

Richard Bolden is Professor of Leadership and Management and Director of Bristol Leadership Centre, University of the West of England, UK.

Morgen Witzel is a writer, lecturer and consultant on leadership and management. He is also a Fellow of the Centre for Leadership Studies, University of Exeter, UK.

Nigel Linacre is a co-founder of Extraordinary Leadership Ltd and is an affiliate of the Centre for Leadership Studies, University of Exeter, UK.

Finally, a leadership text which reveals the paradoxical and messy reality of leadership rather than providing over simplified 'how to' recipes. Bolden, Witzel and Linacre have produced a radical text which is a must-read for the serious student of leadership.

Donna Ladkin, *Professor of Leadership and Ethics, Plymouth University, UK*

Elegantly written throughout, and deeply rooted in both research and practice, each chapter offers novel variations on the central theme of paradox. This is a thought provoking and refreshing antidote to numerous damaging myths about leadership.

Dennis Tourish, *Professor of Leadership and Organization Studies, Royal Holloway University of London, UK*

The early part of the twenty-first century, to date, has been rife with complexity, uncertainty, ambiguity, and unpredictability. One of the inevitable products of the dynamics of our age is the ongoing creation of seemingly thorny, insoluble paradoxes. One cannot lead well without being able to comprehend paradoxes, and to artfully navigate them in ways that edify the group of people one leads. This topic is largely neglected in leadership courses – both in business schools and in broader leadership development efforts in industry and government. This book is an excellent response to this deficit, and a worthy introduction for students and managers who desire to increase their 'paradox navigation' skills as leaders.

Mark E. Mendenhall, *Ph.D., J. Burton Frierson Chair of Excellence in Business Leadership, University of Tennessee, Chattanooga, USA*

Another strikingly original text to come out of the Exeter Centre for Leadership Studies and its wide circle of contacts. Adding something new to a crowded field is not easy, but this distinguished band have done it again!

Stephanie Jones, *Associate Professor, Organizational Behavior, Maastricht School of Management, the Netherlands*

leadershipparadoxes.com

LEADERSHIP PARADOXES

Rethinking leadership for an uncertain world

Edited by Richard Bolden, Morgen Witzel and Nigel Linacre

LONDON AND NEW YORK

First published 2016
by Routledge
2 Park Square, Milton Park, Abingdon, Oxon OX14 4RN

and by Routledge
711 Third Avenue, New York, NY 10017

Routledge is an imprint of the Taylor & Francis Group, an informa business

British Library Cataloguing in Publication Data
A catalogue record for this book is available from the British Library

Library of Congress Cataloging in Publication Data
Leadership paradoxes : rethinking leadership for an uncertain world / edited by Richard Bolden, Morgen Witzel and Nigel Linacre. — First Edition.
pages cm
Includes bibliographical references and index.
1. Leadership. I. Bolden, Richard, editor. II. Witzel, Morgen, editor. III. Linacre, Nigel, editor.
HD57.7.L434345 2016
658.4'092—dc23
2015034355

ISBN: 978-1-138-80711-2 (hbk)
ISBN: 978-1-138-80712-9 (pbk)
ISBN: 978-1-315-75128-3 (ebk)

Typeset in Bembo
by Swales & Willis Ltd, Exeter, Devon, UK

One must not think slightingly of the paradoxical . . .
for the paradox is the source of the thinker's passion,
and the thinker without a paradox
is like a lover without feeling:
a paltry mediocrity.

Søren Kierkegaard

CONTENTS

ILLUSTRATIONS

Figures

Table

Boxes

CONTRIBUTORS

Inmaculada Adarves-Yorno is a Senior Lecturer in Leadership at the University of Exeter Business School. She has more than 20 years of psychology background and is particularly interested in the interface between the inner and the outer world of leadership where paradoxes lie. She has experience as a CEO Advisor of an engineering company and has worked as an Organisational Psychologist. Her current research revolves around change agency, social identity, authentic leadership and mindfulness. In the last five years she has developed authentic leaders and change agents in a range of contexts (including in Kenyan prisons). Some of her latest work was presented in her TEDx talk at the Imperial College London 'Mindful Acceleration'.

Scott Allison has authored numerous books, including *Heroes and Heroic Leadership*. He is Professor of Psychology at the University of Richmond where he has published extensively on heroism and leadership. His other books include *Reel Heroes*, *Conceptions of Leadership*, *Frontiers in Spiritual Leadership* and the *Handbook of Heroism*. His work has appeared in *USA Today*, National Public Radio, the *New York Times*, the *Los Angeles Times*, *Slate Magazine*, MSNBC, CBS,

Psychology Today and the *Christian Science Monitor*. He has received Richmond's Distinguished Educator Award and the Virginia Council of Higher Education's Outstanding Faculty Award.

Jennifer Board is a widely experienced international Human Resources professional with over 30 years' insight into a variety of industries. Beginning her career as an army officer, she then worked in retail, broadcasting and manufacturing before moving into financial services. She held board positions and led large global and regional teams for many years and developed considerable experience in leading the Human Capital aspects of acquisitions, divestitures, restructuring and major change initiatives, working directly with top business leaders. She has lived and worked in New York, Hong Kong, Singapore and London, and has a comprehensive understanding of strategic challenges facing large international businesses. During this time, she was appointed as a Non-Executive Director of the School Teachers Review Body, an independent review body advising government on the pay, terms and conditions of c. 520,000 school teachers in England and Wales. She is a Fellow of the Institute of Directors, an Honorary Fellow of the Centre for Leadership Studies at Exeter University and a Trustee and Chair of the HR/Remuneration Committee for St Margaret's Somerset Hospice.

Richard Bolden is Professor of Leadership and Management and Director of Bristol Leadership Centre at the University of the West of England. His research interests include distributed leadership, systems leadership, leadership in higher education, public-sector leadership, worldly leadership and leadership development evaluation. He is Associate Editor of the journal *Leadership*, Fellow of the Lancaster Leadership Centre and Research Advisor to the Institute of Leadership and Organisation Development, Singapore Civil Service College. Publications include *Exploring Leadership: Individual, Organizational and Society* (with Hawkins, Gosling and Taylor; Oxford University Press, 2011).

Jennifer Cecilione graduated summa cum laude from the University of Richmond in 2015 and holds a BA in psychology with departmental honours. During her time there she worked in Dr Scott Allison's

Hero Lab designing and implementing research studies. She also analysed and presented research findings at the first and second annual Hero Roundtable conferences with Dr Scott Allison. Jennifer now lives in Richmond, VA, and works as a teaching assistant in a school for children who have Autism Spectrum Disorder. She plans to attend graduate school in the near future to study psychology further.

Jeff Gold is Professor of Organisation Learning at Leeds Beckett University, Visiting Professor at Portsmouth University and York St John University. He is a strong advocate of the need for actionable knowledge that is rigorously developed but relevant for practice. He has designed and delivered a wide range of seminars, programmes and workshops on talent management and development, change, strategic learning, futures and foresight, management and leadership development with a particular emphasis on participation and distribution. He is the co-author of CIPD's *Leadership and Management Development* (with Richard Thorpe and Alan Mumford), *The Gower Handbook of Leadership and Management Development* (with Richard Thorpe and Alan Mumford), *Human Resource Development* (with Julie Beardwell, Paul Iles, Rick Holden and Jim Stewart) and *Human Resource Management* (with John Bratton).

John Lawler was Senior Lecturer in Public Service Management at the Centre for International Development at the University of Bradford. He has published works on leadership and management development both generally and specifically in the context of public service organisations.

Nigel Linacre is the author of *The Successful Executive* and an *Introduction to 3-Dimensional Leadership*. As co-founder of Extraordinary Leadership, he works with senior executives in many countries enabling them to develop themselves as leaders, and as co-founder of LeadNow he runs leadership workshops in many universities. His other titles include *Why You Are Here – Briefly* and *The Other Side of You*. An Affiliate of the Centre for Leadership Studies he is also co-founder and Chair of WellBoring, a charity which provides sustainable water solutions for school-based communities, mainly in East Africa.

Morgen Witzel is a Fellow of the Centre for Leadership Studies, University of Exeter Business School in the UK. A writer, lecturer and consultant on leadership and management, especially the history of management, he is the author or co-author of 22 books including *Doing Business in China*, *Management: The Basics* and *A History of Management Thought*, all published by Routledge, as well as the best-selling *Tata: The Evolution of a Corporate Brand*, a profile of India's Tata Group. Morgen lectures at a number of institutions including the University of Exeter, where he teaches on the One-Planet MBA Programme. He has published articles in a variety of academic and popular periodicals and newspapers including the *Financial Times*, the *Toronto Globe & Mail*, the *Los Angeles Times*, *The Smart Manager*, *Financial World* and many others.

PREFACE

It seems somehow appropriate that a book about paradoxes should have its origins in a coincidence. A chance conversation between Roger Niven, then a Fellow of the Centre for Leadership Studies (CLS) at the University of Exeter Business School, and Bob MacKenzie, one of the editors of the journal *e-Organisations and People*,[1] led to an invitation to CLS members to edit and contribute to a special issue of the journal on the subject of leadership. After a short discussion with Bob and his co-editor David McAra, the editors of this book, Morgen Witzel, Richard Bolden and Nigel Linacre, volunteered to edit the special issue.

We had a journal and we had editors, but what was the special issue to be about? 'Leadership' is of course a vast subject, and unless we narrowed the focus considerably there was a risk that we could end up with a collection of articles that had little, if any, relationship with each other. For various reasons, all three of us were very much interested in the idea of paradox, and more specifically, how paradoxes affect leadership and leaders. Casting around, we found that while the subject had been discussed before, the coverage was limited and there seemed plenty of room to make some new contributions. More to the point, we found other authors interested in the subject and happy to write about it.

There was, we freely admit, nothing scientific about the selection of authors. The initial call for papers was limited to members of the CLS academic staff and professional network. Once we had an overview of what content we could expect from CLS we invited selected outside contributors from our own personal networks, people who we knew (a) had an interest in the subject and (b) could write and deliver an article in the specified, fairly short time frame. Our other main concern was to strike the right balance between theory and practice. CLS had a strong reputation in both the academic and practitioner worlds, and indeed, part of its mandate was to bridge the gap between theory and practice and find a forum wherein the two could inform and influence each other. We tried to carry that same approach into the articles for *e-O&P*. Each article had to be rigorous and, where relevant, grounded in theory, but at the same time each had to have something important to say to leadership practitioners.

All this led to quite a subjective approach to article selection, and there are many other people who could have (and perhaps should have) been invited to contribute. Space and time proved to be the final arbitrators, and sadly we had to leave aside some potentially excellent contributions where authors had too many other commitments to allow them to complete on time, and others that we felt duplicated too closely articles already selected for inclusion. The final selection of articles was published in the autumn 2013 issue of *e-O&P* and we would like to take this opportunity once again to thank Bob and David for all their hard work in editing and producing the journal. We hope they were as pleased with the final output as we were.

After publication the question arose: what now? *E-O&P* ran several follow-up discussion sessions, but we felt it would be useful to disseminate these ideas still further. It was at this point that Routledge, our publishers, entered the picture. Would we be willing to edit and expand the articles to form a book? We were, and Bob and David at *e-O&P* gave the project their blessing. Thus this book was born.

The book has a slightly different focus from the original journal issue. First, this book is directed more at students of leadership than practising leaders (although in many cases we expect readers will be both). That meant that not all the original articles were necessarily appropriate; and those that were selected all needed to be considerably fleshed-out and expanded. Second, not all the original authors were available. We ended with the present collection of nine chapters, which we think preserve – and indeed expand considerably upon – the ideas of the original, and will we hope prove to be stimulating food for thought for anyone looking to enquire further into leadership paradoxes.

This book makes no claims to have all the answers about either leadership or paradox. Most of the chapters presented here, as will quickly be seen, ask more questions than they provide answers. Our aim was to stimulate new thinking and debate, and to encourage more and wider reading and study of paradox and ambiguity and how they impact on leadership (to that end, we have provided reading lists with each chapter which should form a beginning for a programme of future study).

We have also developed a website – leadershipparadoxes.com – which offers further material and also a channel for discussion. We hope that these chapters will stimulate reflection and ideas of your own on the subject of leadership and paradox: if they do, then please feel free to share them with us and other readers through the website. In that way, we can develop a learning community that will take the ideas of this book forward; and maybe then, more answers will start to come.

We would like to thank everyone who has been involved in this project from the beginning. The *e-O&P* team have already been mentioned, but we would also like to thank Nicola Cupit and her team at Routledge for their enthusiasm and support for this book. Finally, we want to thank our fellow authors for their patience and hard work. Our names may appear on the cover, but yours was the endeavour that made this book possible.

Note

1 *e-O&P* is the journal of the Association for Management Education and Development (AMED). For more about *e-O&P*, visit the following website: www.amed.org.uk/page/our-lively-and-engaging. AMED's main page can be found at www.amed.org.uk/.

1

INTRODUCTION

Morgen Witzel, Richard Bolden and Nigel Linacre

This chapter introduces the main themes of this book – beginning with the concept of paradox and its relevance to the study and practice of leadership. Morgen Witzel, Richard Bolden and Nigel Linacre suggest that, in a quest for clarity and simplicity, leaders and their organisations all too often apply the wrong tools to the problems, and propose paradox as an alternative perspective. An overview of the structure of the book, including a brief summary of each chapter is then given, followed by a specific note for students of leadership. The chapter concludes with a number of questions for discussion and reflection.

> **Paradox** *n.* a seemingly absurd though perhaps well-founded statement; self-contradictory or essentially absurd statement; person or thing conflicting with pre-conceived notions of what is reasonable or possible.
>
> *(Oxford English Dictionary)*

Why is leadership so difficult? And it must be difficult; surely there is no other reason why so many organisations around the world are so poorly led. If leadership were easy, anyone could do it and we would have a lot fewer problems in our economy and society. We know leadership is difficult too because despite the publication of more than

20,000 books on leadership over the years, we are still not entirely clear what leadership is, or how it works, or even who leaders are.[1]

It is a truism, too, to state that there is no universally agreed definition of leadership. Put twenty leadership scholars and practitioners into a room and ask them to define leadership, and you will probably get twenty-two definitions (at least two will change their mind during the course of the discussion). How can it be that such a vast body of work has been produced on a subject that no one can define? Is there any other subject (apart from perhaps religion) where so much discussion had produced so little illumination?

This book makes no claim to delivering full and complete answers to those questions. Its purpose, instead, is to suggest that instead of attacking the problems of leadership using the standard tools of Cartesian logic and problem-solving, we should perhaps stand back and consider another way.

One of the problems, we believe, that has so far prevented better understanding of what leadership is, how it works and who leaders are, is that leadership is full of paradoxes. These are features of leadership that defy logical analysis; and, as we and our fellow contributors shall show, understanding these paradoxes is also central to the understanding of leadership. Until leadership scholars, consultants, developers and leaders themselves come to terms with the concept of paradox and incorporate it into thinking and practice, then scholarship will never be able to complete its investigatory task, and leaders will continue to struggle to make a lasting impact on the organisations they are supposed to lead.

The nature of paradox

The logician Willard Quine (1966; see also Orenstein, 1998) grouped paradoxes into three categories:

1. *Veridical* paradoxes, which sound at first to be absurd but in the end turn out to be logically true. Schrödinger's Cat[2] is a famous example of a veridical paradox. Another is Jevons's paradox, which states that increases in efficiency of energy consumption will lead to increases in demand for energy. This sounds wrong: an increase in efficiency ought logically to result in a decrease in consumption.

In fact, increased efficiency often leads to falling energy prices which stimulates demand past the original level (as has happened, for example, with oil over the past twenty years).

2. *Falsidical* paradoxes which appear to be false and, upon analysis, turn out to actually *be* false. Zeno's paradox which states that an arrow travelling towards a target will never actually reach the target – it will travel halfway to the target, then half of the remaining half, then half of the remaining quarter and so on, so that it will always be fractionally short of its destination – sounds logical but in fact is quite wrong; we can see, quite clearly, whether an arrow has hit its target or not.
3. *Antinomy* paradoxes, in which we find two equally logical but contradictory statements that no amount of logical reasoning can dispel. This concept was put to good use by Kant to demonstrate the limits of scientific and philosophical inquiry and is characterised by expressions such as 'there is no absolute truth' (a statement that would be proven true if false and vice versa).

It is these antinomy paradoxes that people find most troublesome (especially in the West; people from East Asian cultures tend to be rather better at understanding these paradoxes). For many people, their first impulse upon being confronted with a paradox is to try to 'resolve' it, to render down the conflicting statements so that they agree and the apparent contradiction can be made to go away. We are hard-wired to regard anything difficult as a problem needing to be fixed.

Elsewhere, paradoxes thrive. Western observers of China's economic development have often remarked on the paradoxes they see there, such as the fact that China professes to be a communist state and yet has a capitalist economy (the Communist Party of China is more popular than ever, with nearly eighty-eight million members in 2014, more than double the total at any point during the regime of Mao Zedong (Xinhua, 2014)). One of the most profound remarks ever made about China by an outside observer was Stephen King-Hall's (1927) comment that any statement made about China is both true and, simultaneously, not true. His point was that China is a complex place and cannot be described in simple statements. This is still true today. We can say, for example, that China is an economic superpower (it is the world's second largest economy) and that China is a developing economy (one in six of its population live in absolute poverty). Both statements are true (and to take King-Hall's point, both are therefore not true). It might be possible to reconcile both statements to come up with a single agreeable statement, but in doing so, a great deal of richness of understanding would be lost.

Let us take an example a little closer to home where leadership is concerned, the issue of stress. Stress has been blamed, and still is blamed, for many workplace problems including poor employee mental and physical health, low productivity and low quality (see, for example, Deming, 1986). Leaders are urged to do all they can to reduce stress, to 'drive out fear' in Deming's famous phrase, in the belief that stress-free workplaces will be more productive and more efficient. But this has been questioned repeatedly by others, including Handy (1976), who argue that an element of stress can make people *more* productive and *more* efficient, literally keeping them on their toes. Eliminating stress altogether, attractive though it might sound, can also eliminate the push factors that lead people to perform and excel. The stress paradox, sometimes also called the self-absorption paradox, suggests that people need to experience a degree of discomfort in order to perform effectively; what is bad for them is, at the same time, also good for them.

It could be argued that one of the tasks for the leader is not to eliminate stress but to understand the paradox and work out where exactly the optimal level is;[3] to identify the fine line where stress ceases to be a positive externality and turns into a negative one. Instead, though, much of the popular work on managing people – featured in trade magazines, on blogs, in professional conferences – continues to follow the Deming route and urges the elimination of stress.

The central point to be made about antinomy paradoxes is this: they are not puzzles to be solved or opposites that can be reconciled. They simply *are*. Rather than dissecting them, we need to learn to accept them as wholes and learn to live with them and manage them. Yet Western people, in particular, tend to be very bad at doing this.

The wrong tools for the wrong problems

When seeking a better understanding of leadership, it is important to recall the advice of the Irish postmaster to the lost motorist seeking the road to Dublin that 'you can't get there from here'. We are attempting to analyse a necessarily complex phenomenon using a set of tools designed to make things simple, using the wrong tools to solve what are very likely the wrong problems as well.

As Hodgson (2007) and others have remarked, the vast majority of leadership theory over the past fifty years has emanated from American research establishments, and most of what remains has come from northern Europe: the UK primarily, but also France, Germany and Scandinavia. Witzel (2012) has noted how there is virtually no original theorising on leadership in management coming out of Asia today, despite the vast richness of leadership literature in those regions from antiquity; most of the work that has been published is derivative and based on Western thinking with little attempt at cultural context (there are a few honourable exceptions, of course).

Living with an antinomy paradox requires us to do something which is, in descriptive terms, quite simple: accept that there is no black and white, no right and wrong, and that two or more logically incompatible positions might well be true – yet, in reality, most of us find this difficult. Partly this is because, as Witzel (2012) points out, Western thinking about management has been heavily conditioned over the past hundred years by the Taylorist concept of the 'one best way'; there is only one 'best' way of doing things and all others are inferior. Taylorism tends to push us into narrow channels of thinking reliant on Cartesian logic and step-by-step approaches.

And Cartesian logic is, to repeat the phrase, the wrong tool. Cartesian logic is very good at breaking problems down into their component parts and working out cause and effect. But when there is a discontinuity between cause and effect, or when the cause leads to multiple and contradictory effects, our logical tools break down. In terms of analysing leadership, it may be that cause-and-effect analysis has taken us about as far as we can go. It is time, perhaps past time, that we stopped and stood back and looked at leadership not as a series of problems that can be solved, but as a series of contradictory, puzzling and obscure concepts that need to be managed and lived with. The purpose of this work, then, is to introduce some of the paradoxes of leadership and to suggest some ways that leaders and organisations may learn to live with them (although we make no claim whatsoever to complete coverage of either of these subjects).

Structure of the book

We begin this book by looking at paradoxes that affect how we think about leadership and define it and how we view leaders. Morgen Witzel suggests that there is a paradox at the heart of our definition of leadership. It is generally accepted that people *need* leaders, but do they *want* them? This chapter argues that there is a tension inherent in our attitudes towards leadership, and that even as we accept the control that leaders have over us we also kick back against it and try to assert our own control over our leaders. Richard Bolden continues this line of argument through an exploration of the paradoxes faced when researching leadership. In particular, he suggests, there is an enduring tension between individual and collective perspectives on leaders, leading and leadership that results in us frequently looking in the wrong places for the wrong kinds of evidence.

These paradoxes of understanding lead in turn to paradoxes in the practice of leadership. Nigel Linacre suggests that leaders are also caught in a spatial and temporal paradox that requires them to be both 'here' and 'elsewhere'. Leaders must be part of the group; but at the same time, their status as leaders sets them apart. And leaders must manage in the present; but at the same time, they must also think constantly about the future. Scott Allison and Jennifer Cecilione go on to describe the often paradoxical ways that we create heroes out of our leaders, and note that whilst we may all agree on the idea of heroism, we usually have quite different ideas about who our heroes are. Strangely, the heroes that most people agree have heroic status are often characters from fiction. We also tend to ascribe heroic status to people only once they have gone. Thus our only truly heroic leaders are either dead, or never existed at all.

Paradox also has implications for leaders themselves, and paradoxes are responsible for many of the strains and stresses placed on them. John Lawler and Jeff Gold argue that most leaders don't really understand how leadership works, and that they don't really control what they lead. Most leaders operate in a 'fog' in which their sense of control is often illusory. These limitations clearly offer a challenge to common understandings of what it means to lead. Inmaculada Adarves-Yorno takes up a similar question in relation to the concept of authentic leadership, and finds that this too places paradoxical demands and expectations on leaders. Feeling the pressure to be authentic, leaders may find themselves needing to adopt inauthentic behaviours and actions in order to make themselves *seem* more authentic; in effect, they learn how to fake sincerity. Finally, Jennifer Board considers the idea of moral courage, often described as an essential attribute of leadership, and asks whether this is always true. There may be times when moral courage requires leaders to turn a blind eye to 'wrong' in order to achieve the 'right' result. She cautions that while necessary, judgements about the ethics of leadership can be dangerous and frequently misleading.

The book concludes by highlighting some of the key themes raised throughout and considering their implications for leadership theory, practice and development over the coming years. While leadership and in particular leadership development would be easier if we were all the same and so could lead in the same way, we all turn out to be different, and these differences amongst us will be reflected in the way that we lead. Discovering how you can best lead is a job only you can do.

It is our hope that these chapters will provide useful food for thought and discussion in your own leadership thinking, learning and practice. We hope, too, that the publication of this book is not a one-way street. We encourage you to contact us through the book's website, and look forward to hearing your own thoughts and experiences of paradox. Of course, one of the implications of Heisenberg's uncertainty principle is that the more we study a subject the less precise our knowledge of it becomes. But maybe this is a case where we need less knowledge, and more understanding.

'The supreme paradox of all thought is the attempt to discover something that thought cannot think', wrote the philosopher Søren Kierkegaard. 'This passion is at bottom present in all thinking, even in the thinking of the individual, in so far as in thinking he participates in something transcending himself.' Logical thinking is critically important, for leaders as for everyone around them. But not everything submits itself to logic; think for example of transcendence. We can use paradox as a tool to understand the realms of thought and sense where logic cannot take us. If the chapters in this book do nothing else, they show us that there is more – much more – to leadership than conventional understanding would have us believe.

A note for students of leadership

Whilst this book is written for a broad audience we would like to conclude this chapter with some specific advice for those reading it as part of a taught course or programme of study. For such readers the need to demonstrate their learning through written and/or practical assignments is likely to be of particular concern; and will be assessed against criteria such as critical thinking, reflection, integration of theory and practice, and engagement with a wider body of literature. This book has been written with these points in mind and each chapter is supported by a number of questions for discussion and reflection (either individually or in groups; in or outside of class) as well as recommendations for further reading. There is also a companion website with additional resources, including short videos from the contributors and links to useful resources.

This, however, is not a traditional textbook. Rather than providing a definitive set of concepts to be learnt and applied the ideas within each chapter should be taken as provocations and catalysts for further enquiry. As the famous saying goes: 'you get out what you put in'. By assimilating the contents of this book you will learn a number of things, but not nearly as much as you will learn by questioning, challenging, testing and further exploring the ideas in relation to your own experience, aspirations and context (organisational, cultural, professional, etc.).

This book also differs from more traditional textbooks through the way(s) in which we engage with theory in relation to practice. Our aim is to illustrate the lived experience of leadership and how this informs, and is informed by, mental models and assumptions about the dynamics of power, influence and identity, rather than to explore leadership theory per se. In order to do this, whilst we engage with a range of theories and concepts such as leader–follower relations (Chapter 2), distributed leadership (Chapter 3), team leadership (Chapter 4), heroic leadership (Chapter 5), leadership traits and styles (Chapter 6), authentic leadership (Chapter 7) and ethical leadership (Chapter 8), by-and-large these concepts are addressed indirectly, through a problem-centred approach, rather than as discrete concepts to be studied and analysed in their own right. For more detail and explanation of particular theories, including their strengths and limitations, you will need to refer to other sources including, but not limited to, those in the recommended reading section of each chapter.

The overall framing of this book is around leadership in contexts of complexity and uncertainty. There may well be times when leadership is far more straightforward than this book might suggest – for example where the nature of the task is clearly delineated and there is widespread agreement about the best way forward – but even in apparently simple situations leadership is often contested and elusive. Keith Grint, a well-renowned UK leadership scholar, recalls that when he first started studying leadership following a successful career outside of higher education he was pretty sure of what he knew about leadership. A few years later, after much research and enquiry, he realised that he was far less certain of what he knew about leadership than before. Whilst many would despair of this fact – regarding those years of work as a futile endeavour – Grint saw it as a sure sign that he was beginning to make progress, testament to his growing understanding of the socially constructed nature of this concept and the complex processes through which we come recognise and describe certain things, and not others, as leadership (see Grint, 2010, pp. 1–4).

By exploring the ideas in this book, we hope that you too will gain a greater appreciation of the breadth and depth of leadership studies and begin to recognise the limitations, and precarious foundations, of much existing knowledge. As Joanne Ciulla argues in the conclusion to the book *The Quest for a General Theory of Leadership* (summarising the outcomes of a five-year process of enquiry and debate between an interdisciplinary group of leading US leadership scholars):

> It takes more than one scholar, discipline, or theoretical approach to understand leadership. The study of leadership forces us to tackle the universal questions about human nature and destiny. For those questions, there will probably never be a general theory.
>
> *(Ciulla, 2006, p. 233)*

Questions for reflection and discussion

1. Consider the following paradox: a thing can be both right and wrong at the same time. Do you think this is true? Can you think of any examples in your own work, or life? Do you find that you are comfortable living with and working with paradoxes, or do you find them an irritant, something that you want to resolve or make go away?

2. Think about leadership as you have experienced it and/or studied it. What kinds of paradoxes might leaders face? Make a list of as many as you can. If you are working in a group, suggest to your colleagues that they do the same, and then compare your lists and discuss.
3. 'The supreme paradox of all thought is the attempt to discover something that thought cannot think.' What does this mean to you?
4. How do different cultures perceive leadership? Do Chinese and Indian people have different perceptions and expectations of leadership from Europeans or Americans? You may need to do some research on this; when you have completed your research tasks, list as many cultural differences in perceptions of leadership theory and practice as you can.
5. And following on from this, from your experience or your studies, can you think of any situations or concepts which leaders from one culture might find paradoxical and uncomfortable, but leaders from another culture might regard as normal?

Notes

1 The estimate of 20,000 was made by Grint (2006) and has certainly increased since then. A recent search on Amazon showed over 110,000 titles, some of which may discuss leadership only tangentially.

2 A thought experiment designed by the Austrian physicist Edwin Schrödinger to demonstrate a principle of quantum mechanics that requires two competing suppositions (in this case that a cat in a sealed box is both dead and alive) to be maintained until an empirical observation can be made to verify which is correct.

3 Leadership scholar and consultant Ron Heifetz calls this the 'zone of productive disequilibrium' (Heifetz *et al.*, 2009).

Recommended reading

Grint, K. (2010) *Leadership: A Very Short Introduction*, Oxford: Oxford University Press.

Heifetz, R., Grashow, A. and Linsky, M. (2009) *The Practice of Adaptive Leadership: Tools and Tactics for Changing your Organisation and the World*, Boston, MA: Harvard Business Press.

Quine, Willard V. (1966) *The Ways of Paradox and Other Essays*, New York, NY: Random House.

Sorenson, Roy (2005) *A Brief History of the Paradox: Philosophy and Labyrinths of the Mind*, Oxford: Oxford University Press.

Witzel, Morgen (2012) *A History of Management Thought*, London: Routledge; 2nd edn forthcoming, 2016.

References

Ciulla, J. (2006) 'What we learned along the way: a commentary', in G.R. Goethals and G.L.J. Sorenson (eds) *The Quest for a General Theory of Leadership*, Cheltenham: Edward Elgar, pp. 221–233.

Deming, W. Edwards (1986) *Out of the Crisis*, Cambridge, MA: MIT Center for Advanced Engineering Study.

Grint, Keith (2006) 'Foreword', in Jonathan Gosling, Peter Case and Morgen Witzel (eds) *John Adair: Fundamentals of Leadership*, Basingstoke: Palgrave Macmillan, p. xi.

Grint, K. (2010) *Leadership: A Very Short Introduction*, Oxford: Oxford University Press.

Handy, Charles (1976) *Understanding Organisations*, London: Penguin.

Heifetz, R., Grashow, A. and Linsky, M. (2009) *The Practice of Adaptive Leadership: Tools and Tactics for Changing your Organisation and the World*, Boston, MA: Harvard Business Press.

Hodgson, Phil (2007) 'In search of European leadership', *European Business Forum* 30: 32–35.

King-Hall, Stephen (1927) *China of To-Day*, London: Woolf.

Orenstein, Alex (1998) 'Quine, Willard Van Orman', in Edward Craig (ed.) *Routledge Encyclopedia of Philosophy*, London: Routledge, vol. 8, pp. 3–14.

Quine, Willard V. (1966) *The Ways of Paradox and Other Essays*, New York, NY: Random House.

Witzel, Morgen (2012) *A History of Management Thought*, London: Routledge; 2nd edn forthcoming, 2016.

Xinhua News Agency (2014) 'CPC has 87.79 mln members', available at: www.china.org.cn/china/2015-06/29/content_35939304.htm.

2

THE FIRST PARADOX OF LEADERSHIP IS – LEADERSHIP!

Morgen Witzel

The notion that 'people want to be led' is deep-seated in much of modern leadership practice, even if leadership theorists are prone to express doubts. In this chapter Morgen Witzel suggests that this may be a misconception – one, moreover, with serious consequences. While it is true that leaders require the consent of the led, it is too often assumed that this consent, once given, cannot or will not be revoked and that followers will support leaders because they genuinely desire that others should lead them. Witzel argues instead that people may accept the need *for leadership, but that in most cases they accept leaders out of necessity rather than true desire. This chapter goes on to explore some ways of dealing with the paradox of need and want, and what the implications might be for leaders in business, politics and elsewhere.*

Leadership is something that nearly everyone needs, but hardly anyone wants. True, many people want to be leaders, for a variety of reasons both selfish and altruistic (though it should also be recognised that many others, the present author included, do not want to be leaders), but very few people genuinely desire to be led. At best, they accept the obligations of followership reluctantly, and if leaders begin to take them in directions they do not wish to go, they will object, often quite vigorously, and then attempt to subvert or overthrow the leaders placed over them.

The paradox is this: we do not *want* leadership, but we know that we *need* it. As human beings and part of an organised society, we understand the need for leadership. Leaders enable us to do things that we know we could not do on our own; they provide a vital ingredient in the organisations that are the building blocks of our civilisations, both Western and Eastern: businesses, government, the state, the armed forces, even our leisure organisations such as sports teams and golf clubs will in the vast majority of circumstances require leaders to give them cohesion and direction. Organisations that function effectively without leaders do exist, but they are very rare.

As human beings, as members of a society, we welcome the *idea* of leadership and know, subconsciously if not consciously, that accepting a leader involves handing over an element of our independence; we surrender partial control of our actions to other people in exchange for what leaders bring to us: special skills, special knowledge, symbolic power. We accept that leaders can place boundaries on our actions, and can ask or even order us to do things that we might not have thought of doing ourselves. But here is the paradox: just as we accept the authority that leaders place over us as a necessity, we also – again, subconsciously if not consciously – resent that authority and push back against it. Just as our leaders place boundaries on us, so too we attempt to place boundaries on them, limiting their authority over us.

We may accept that our bosses have strong power over what we do in the workplace, but we would kick back strongly against any attempt to control what we do outside of the workplace; the current debate over the rights of firms to control what their employees can post on Facebook is an example of this (Carlin, 2011). We accept the authority of the state in certain spheres of our lives, but reject it utterly in others; again, the ongoing debate over privacy, specifically referring to the government's right to intercept mobile phone and Internet communications, is an example (*Guardian,* 2012).

But the paradox also runs much deeper, to the level of support we give our leaders in their designated sphere of activity. We accept the authority of leaders only so long as their wishes and needs coincide with our own. We support our leaders only so long as they do what we want them to do, and when they begin to take action that is against our wishes – even when it is in our best interests – we turn against them. Leaders must live, every day, with the paradox that although leadership is an essential feature of organisational life – we could even say, an essential feature of civilisation – most people resent the authority that leaders represent, and once that resentment reaches a certain level they will, passively or even actively, begin to work against their leaders. This is true in the workplace, in civil society, even in the armed forces.

In this chapter, I will discuss this *paradox of need and rejection* in a little more detail and then look at three attempts to resolve the paradox by three different authors: Laozi (or Lao Tzu), the ancient Chinese sage and author of the *Daodejing*, the French Enlightenment philosopher Jean-Jacques Rousseau in his book *Of the Social Contract*, and the American scholar John Kotter in perhaps his best-known work *A Force for Change* (1990). I have picked these three because they represent very different times and places and cultures, and show that awareness of this paradox has been alive and well for a very long time. All three of these attempts shed light on the paradox, but none is ultimately successful in resolving it, for reasons I will come onto at the end of the chapter. Before we begin, let us look first at how people reject leadership, and how at the same time traditional leadership theory often assumes passive acceptance.

There go my people!

In 1793, a few years after the outbreak of the French Revolution, a counter-revolution erupted in western France in the area known as the Vendée. The rebels rejected the ideals of the French Revolution and were determined on armed resistance, but none had military experience and they lacked a leader who could organise a campaign and give them direction. They identified a local nobleman, François de Charette, who had been an officer in the French army before the revolution, and decided he should be their leader (Ross, 1975).

For his part, Charette had no interest in leading a rebellion; he foresaw (correctly, as it turned out) that the uprising was doomed to failure. When the rebels came to his house, he told his servants to tell them he was away from home. Undeterred, the rebels returned several times, on one occasion searching the house; Charette only escaped from his would-be followers by hiding under his bed.

Eventually the rebels caught up with him and forced the reluctant Charette to be their leader. He duly did as they asked, leading a rebel army to ambush a government supply convoy. But when he ordered his followers to capitalise on this victory and advance, they refused. They had done what they set out to do; they had fought a battle against the government and won. Now they were going home, and Charette could do whatever he liked (Ross, 1975).

The story of Charette – which is by no means unique in history – suggests that we may need to think again about the relationship between leaders and followers. Traditionally, that relationship has been portrayed in a somewhat top-down, paternalistic way. This is true even into the modern period. Burns (1978), arguably the founding father of the concept of transformational leadership, described leadership as a process where leaders arouse and engage their followers, 'lifting' followers to make them into 'better selves'. The leader is proactive, the followers largely passive until the leader engages with them and 'transforms' them. Bennis (1989) thought that one of the attributes of a leader was the ability to inspire others; leaders create vision and then bring other people to share that vision so that they can work together to reach a goal.

Even Greenleaf's concept of 'servant leadership' occasionally falls into the trap of assuming that leaders should fulfil the duty of guiding the organisation, and that while caring for others and meeting their needs, it is down to the leader to determine what those needs are (Greenleaf, 1977).

This proactive view of leadership runs into a roadblock, however, when we understand that the so-called 'followers' very often have views of their own, and visions of their own. They have their own set ideas of what they want out of life. They look for leaders, not to give them goals, but to help them reach more effectively the goals they already have.

'There go my people!' cried a Roman senator, rushing down the street following a mob of protesting citizens. 'I must go after them, so I can find out where they want me to lead them!' The story is (probably) apocryphal, but it nonetheless illustrates the problem of what happens when visions collide. The senator, at least, was self-aware enough to realise that it was the will of the people, not his own will, that dictated what would happen next. More commonly, leaders – naturally enough, for their training has assured them that *they* are the ones with the vision – resent the appearance of a competing vision and try to crush it or push it aside, thereby imposing their own will on the organisation. This includes not only formally appointed leaders but those who emerge from the ranks; Adolf Hitler is an excellent example. Sometimes, indeed, they are right to do so; we can think of turnarounds of toxic organisations, failing businesses like IBM or failing sports teams or governments where a strong leader manages to swim against the tide and create success where before there had been failure.

Less commonly noted and far less commonly studied are the cases where the leader fails to make an impact on the organisation and is forced out by his or her followers. The resignation of Euan Sutherland as CEO of the Co-operative Group in 2014 after he failed to make headway against an entrenched corporate culture, or the failure of the leader of the Liberal Democrat Party in the UK, Nick Clegg, to persuade his followers that he had done the right thing in entering into a governing coalition with the Conservatives after the 2010 general election, are cases in point.

Leaders: a necessary evil

Despite countless cases of leaders failing to make an impact on organisations, even of leaders being driven out of organisations when people rebel against them, the view persists amongst leaders themselves that people 'want' to be led, and that without leadership people cannot survive or prosper. The bold statement attributed to Jim Quigley, former CEO of Deloitte, that 'people want to be led', is often recited and repeated – not least in the management coaching and consultancy fraternities – as if by repetition the statement will somehow become true. Rather more rare is the observation by Goffee and Jones (2007) that 'if clever people have one defining characteristic, it is that they do not want to be led'.

'The more we talked . . . the clearer it became that the psychological relationship leaders have with their clever people is very different from the one they have with traditional followers', Goffee and Jones continue. 'Clever' people want freedom; they want to be treated as equals with the leaders; and they want recognition for what they have done. Goffee and Jones hit on the nub of the issue when they state that 'clever people need the organization as much as it needs them'. People join organisations, in other words, because they need the organisation's help to achieve their goals; but if the organisation will not, or cannot, help them, then they will leave.

But why stop at so-called 'clever' people? It is time we recognised that everyone, not just elites, joins an organisation in order to satisfy needs of their own. In the world of work we have a tradition of studies stretching back to the Hawthorne experiments in the 1920s (Mayo, 1933) that confirms this. Sometimes, those needs are simple. Especially in developing countries, people may go to work simply in order to make enough money to satisfy physical needs for food, shelter and safety. Rama Bijapurkar (2008) identifies a unit of workers of this type in India, which she calls 'the resigned'. Their goal, their purpose, is to survive, and very little else will engage their attention unless and until their physical needs are met. There is little point in attempting to motivate them towards higher things; they are already very highly motivated by the need to survive, and they will fight anyone who stands in the way of that need.

Others, though, go to work for a variety of reasons, one of the most important of which is the social need for 'belongingness', the need to be part of a group of people where we feel at home and valued (Maslow, 1954). We go to work, in other words, to enjoy the society of other people like ourselves, and our loyalty to them is paramount (at least, so long as they demonstrate loyalty to us). This phenomenon can be seen quite clearly in police forces, and the extent to which police officers will cover up for fellow officers accused of wrongdoing, putting the interests of their affinity group over the interests of the organisation. Others seek work that provides them with meaning and makes them feel good about what they do; but as Herzberg (1966) observed, it is they that define what that meaning is, not someone else. The same is true for our motives in joining political parties, sports teams or their fan bases, the armed forces, or even religious groups.

However, the notion that people want to be led has no empirical foundation, and must surely be consigned to the dimension that Mintzberg (1973) referred to as 'folklore', things that we believe to be true about organisations without any foundation of evidence. And evidence that people reject leadership when it does not suit them is there in plenty. Civilisations of every kind, West and East, have a long tradition of celebrating those who defy authority, Robin Hood and the Outlaws of the Marsh being cases in point. Both are legendary, but both show how highly we value our right to rebel.

The same tradition informs our own everyday actions. As noted earlier, when we are at work, we accept what our leaders tell us to do, more or less willingly. But would we allow our bosses to tell us what to do outside of the workplace? Would we allow them to come into our homes and tell us what to eat, or what television programmes to watch? The answer in most cases is, probably not. Certainly when our political leaders try to do exactly that, telling us to eat healthy foods or take more exercise or recycle our plastics, the response from many people is to raise two fingers to the politicians and carry on doing what they want.

As the Wikileaks and Edward Snowden affairs have shown in recent years, there is widespread sympathy with those who defy authority – even though the results in both cases could compromise national security and, in theory, lead to the deaths of other people at some point in the future. Those who leaked government secrets to the newspapers presumably knew this, but acted anyway. Why? Because there is a growing fear in many quarters that governments are becoming too powerful and have too much control over the people. A poll in 2012 showed that nearly two-thirds of Americans believe that the state has too much power (Rasmussen Reports, 2013). Anecdotal evidence from India and China suggests that while people are less discontented with the idea of government, they are increasingly prepared to object to what governments do, and to stand up to their appointed leaders. According to the *Wall Street Journal*, there were 1.5 million labour disputes in China in 2012, many of which have been directed at local government; in 2005, the number was 200,000 (Lubman, 2014).

The United States is an interesting case in point. The American colonies declared independence in 1776, but not until 1787 did the American states grudgingly agree to have a president (Milkis and Nelson, 2008). The first US president, George Washington, faced a series of rebellions against presidential authority. The most serious of these was the Whiskey Rebellion of 1791, ostensibly about taxes but in fact a protest against the imposition of leaders by those who believed that leadership was not necessary (Boyd, 1985). These rebellions were part of a philosophical view very prevalent in American society that leadership was neither necessary nor desirable. Thomas Jefferson – who, ironically, became president himself some years later – declared that subjugating one's own ideas and action to those of a leader was 'the last degradation of a free and moral agent' (Jefferson, 1989). The men who drafted the American constitution were very much aware of this view, and took great care to ensure that the other branches of government, the legislature and the judiciary, could exercise control over the presidency and limit its actions. Even those in favour of presidential leadership were worried about its consequences.

There is a rising belief in both the media and popular culture that the balance of power between followers and leaders is tipping too far towards the latter. 'People should not be afraid of their governments', says a character in the film *V for Vendetta*, 'governments should be afraid of their people'. And of course, this does not just apply to governments. In 2011, the words and actions of Rupert Murdoch and his News International organisation came under intense scrutiny. Ostensibly this was because of alleged illegal news-gathering practices, phone-hacking, but behind this for many lay the fear that Murdoch might be on the verge of becoming 'too powerful', too influential (Thompson, 2015).

Argyris (1957) has described what he calls 'defensive routines', action which members of an organisation take to slow down or derail changes with which they do not agree. Very often, says Argyris, this is because members believe that their leaders do not know what is best; the members themselves are the true custodians of the organisation's values and must act to protect the organisation itself.

It could be argued that this is a Western phenomenon, and that other cultures embrace leadership more willingly. Geert Hofstede's work on culture shows that East Asian cultures have a higher 'power distance' score than those of Britain or the United States, indicating that people are more willing to accept that there is an inequality of power distribution within society (Hofstede, 1980). This is sometimes interpreted as meaning that people are more accepting of or have a great need for strong leadership. A brief scan of the history of China will show that this is not so. From the White Lotus Society in the eighteenth century to the Taipings in the nineteenth and the

Communist Party in the twentieth, China has never lacked movements which sought to control, dominate or even destroy existing systems of leadership. During the Cultural Revolution, Mao Zedong urged the Red Guards to resist their leaders and defy authority (MacFarquhar and Schoenhals, 2006). Another paradox: a leader urging his followers to reject leadership!

It could also be argued that modern people are more sceptical and hence more resistant to leadership and that in an earlier more deferential age people accepted their leaders unquestioningly. I very much doubt whether that age ever existed. Let us take just one example, the church, where it is commonly assumed that until modern times people were humble and full of piety, churches were full every Sunday and vicars were respected authority figures. But the correspondence of vicars in the eighteenth century is full of complaints about empty churches, with attendance on Sundays often no more than one or two people despite repeated warnings that failure to attend church could lead to eternal damnation. In southern Germany in the fifteenth century, clergy were driven out of their parishes entirely by people angry over perceived abuses in the church (Scribner, 1987). One could ride for hundreds of miles across Bavaria and not see a single tenanted church. Rejection of leadership is not a new phenomenon.

How then to deal with people who do not want to be led, even though they may need leadership – and may even recognise that need, while simultaneously resenting it? There have been several approaches to the paradox over time, and we will now turn to discussing three of them.

Laissez-faire leadership

The *Daodejing* (or *Tao Teh Ching* (literally, *The Book of the Way and Virtue*)), ascribed to the sixth-century-BC Chinese sage Laozi, is one of the classics of Chinese philosophy and remains widely read and admired. Unlike his more authoritarian contemporaries, Confucius and Han Fei, Laozi argued that strong leadership was bad for people and bad for society. Authoritarian leadership was, for Laozi, an artificial construct, one that ran contrary to the natural order of things. More pragmatically, it was also not a very effective way of getting things done. People disliked being told what to do by their leaders; they wanted to be free, to act according to their own wishes and to take responsibility for their actions (all quotes taken from Wu, 1990).

> The highest type of ruler is one of whose existence the people are barely aware.
> Next comes one whom they love and praise.
> Next comes one whom they fear.
> Next comes one whom they despise and defy.

Laozi tried to deal with the paradox of need and rejection by introducing the principle of *wu-wei*, or 'non-action' (later translated by French Jesuit scholars as *laissez-faire*, this is now a core principle in modern economic thought). *Wu-wei* should not be confused with 'inaction' or doing nothing at all. Another translation might be 'non-intervention'. According to Laozi the ruler should trust the people to know what is right and act accordingly. He also invokes the principle of *dao*, what we might call natural law. Leave things alone, do not interfere, and the right result will occur naturally.

> The Sage is self-effacing and scanty of words.
> When his task is accomplished and things have been completed,
> All the people say: 'We ourselves have achieved it!'

This is not a million miles from John Adair's definition of leadership as 'getting things done through other people, willingly' (Adair, 1989: 23). The extra dimension is that leadership in Laozi's scheme has such a light touch that people do not even notice its existence. And, it follows, we cannot fear or resent or fight back against something whose existence we do not notice. Leaders have experimented with this form of leadership more recently, perhaps the most famous example being Ricardo Semler at Semco who devolved nearly all of his leadership responsibilities to his employees (Semler, 1993).

Laozi's response to the paradox of need and rejection, then, is for the leader to withdraw into the background. Rather than 'actively' leading people through authority and control, he or she merely creates the conditions necessary for other people to take action, then stands back and waits for the grand plan to evolve.

The social contract

There are similarities between the basic views of Laozi and the eighteenth-century French philosopher of the Enlightenment, Jean-Jacques Rousseau. He is perhaps most famous for his statement that 'man is born free, but lives everywhere in chains' (all quotes taken from Rousseau, 1998). Freedom for Rousseau is consistent with the idea of natural law; authority is an artificial construct which is imposed on us, more often than not against our will.

But Rousseau also questions whether the forcible imposition of authority is in fact 'real'. In *The Social Contract*, first published in 1762, Rousseau rejects as illegitimate any authority which we do not accept willingly, but at times he also appears to question whether such authority really exists. Do tyrants truly govern by force, or is it all smoke and mirrors? Do we accept the authority of force only because we have not woken up and realised we can shake off those chains at will? A similar point was made by Manfred Kets de Vries in his excellent book *Lessons on Leadership by Terror*, where he describes the illusions that tyrants must create in order to maintain power; if they knew how truly weak such leaders were, the people would rise up and overthrow them at once (Kets de Vries, 2004).

The only real authority, says Rousseau, is that which derives for ourselves. Merely by acting as individuals, though, we cannot exercise authority effectively. Therefore we voluntarily join forces, surrendering in part our rights as individuals in exchange for the benefits that the community provides us. The agreements that bind us together are what he terms the 'social contract':

> The heart of the social contract may be stated simply. Each of us places his person and authority under the supreme direction of the general will, and the group receives each individual as an indivisible part of the whole.

In Rousseau's thinking, the leader becomes a kind of executive agent, guided by the general will. Instead of the leader imposing himself/herself on the organisation, it is the other way around. The question of how broad the general will is, or should be, is one that needs addressing. During the recent rash of press stories about tax avoidance by large corporations, Google executive Eric Schmidt argued that he and his colleagues were following the will of shareholders, who desired that the company should pay as little tax as possible (*Guardian,* 2013). But in Rousseau's order of things, the will of all stakeholders, not just one group, should be obeyed, remembering that each is an indivisible part of the whole.

Where Laozi pushes leaders into the background, Rousseau draws them into the system and makes them part of it, equal to their followers in status and equally subordinate to the general will. Authority now rests with the followers and not the leaders.

A force for change

John Kotter's *A Force for Change: How Leadership Differs from Management* takes a different approach. Kotter switches the focus back to the leader and what he or she does, but argues for a fundamental redefinition of the tasks of the leader and even of what leadership is (Kotter, 1990; see also Moore and Klein, 2013). Famously, Kotter separates leadership from management. Leadership is about creating vision, creating 'human networks' to achieve the vision, inspiring people to work towards making the vision real, and creating change. Management is about planning, monitoring and control.

Kotter began his research rather where this chapter began, with an awareness that there was a great deal of resistance to change which leaders could not overcome. His response – and as readers of Kotter will know, I am simplifying greatly here – is to shift the focus of leadership towards human relations, towards motivating and inspiring people so as to overcome the barriers to change. Leaders are no longer responsible for authority and control; apart from moral authority, Kotter's leaders do not seem to have much authority at all. They do not sublimate themselves to the general will in the way that Rousseau advises, but there is a strong sense that they are working in partnership with followers.

Meanwhile, all the negative aspects – the nasty yucky stuff that causes dissension and resentment, like control and authority – are the province of managers. There is a strong sense that in a perfect Kotter-esque organisation, should such a thing exist, people would love their leaders but hate their managers. In effect, then, Kotter does a sleight of hand. He takes away the things that people don't like about leadership from the role of the leader, and leaves only the positive motivational and inspirational side. Thus the source of conflict is removed.

Living with the paradox

All three writers offer us interesting solutions. Laozi suggests that leaders should so far as possible let the natural law take its course and the best leadership is as little leadership as possible. Rousseau argues that leaders should be internalised, brought into the organisation and subjected to the general will so that there is no difference between them and followers, with leaders becoming merely executives. Kotter goes in the other direction, seemingly believing that it is the executive function that is the cause of dissent; he separates this out from the role of leadership and urges leaders to concentrate on motivation and relationship building.

All three have their weaknesses. Laozi's *laissez-faire* leaders are unlikely to be able to step up quickly and take charge in a crisis, the time when leadership is often most necessary (a point made by Han Fei in his critique of Laozi) (Witzel, 2012). Rousseau's ideas are the cornerstone of modern Western democracy, but they have been unable to stop leaders from shaking off the general will and imposing themselves on the rest of us (we should never forget that Adolf Hitler came to power in Germany through the democratic process; he was not the only dictator to do so). As my colleague Nigel Linacre reminds me, the notion of the general will has been employed very usefully by dictators claiming to embody that will. And Kotter's well-meaning distinction between leaders and managers has turned into something of a nightmare, with leaders refusing to take control or authority even when it is required of them; I have referred to this elsewhere as 'a lethal cocktail of ignorance and incompetence' (Witzel, 2013).

But are we perhaps expecting too much when we turn to these authorities? A paradox is not a puzzle to be solved or a problem to be got around. A paradox just *is*; it is an essential component of being. The original Daoist paradox of light and darkness showed these not as opposing forces, but as two halves of the same whole. Maybe that is how we need to see the need for leadership and the dislike or rejection of it. We dislike unpleasant or bad-tasting medicine even though we know it will make us feel better; we dislike surrendering control to others, but in our heart of hearts we know this is necessary.

And here, I submit, is the heart of the problem. Attempts to resolve paradoxes are ultimately futile, because genuine paradoxes cannot be resolved. They merely exist. They are inconvenient truths which challenge what we think we know about the world; and in this case, the paradox changes what we think we know about leadership. In particular, the paradox challenges the folkloric idea that 'people want to be led'. People may need leadership, but the paradox of need and rejection suggests that they might need it for quite different reasons than we have traditionally assumed. They need leadership to help them get to where they want to go, be that to climb the highest mountain, or to finish the day with enough money to buy food for their families. Whatever leaders may think, the goals people have set themselves are the most important and will prevail.

Do people need to be inspired? The paradox suggests that what people really need from leaders is help: a rope to climb the mountain, or a job that will earn them the money they need to buy food, or anywhere in between, depending on the person and their situation. This in turn suggests that we need to think again about what it is that leaders really do in order to be effective – as opposed to what they think they do, or what others tell them they should be doing. When people already know what they want, and turn to leaders for help, they are not seeking masters – or servants. They are seeking partners in an enterprise which might mean everything to them; even the difference between life and death.

Rather than trying to find a way around the paradox, we should simply accept it and then use the knowledge of the paradox to become better leaders. Each of the three ways outlined in this chapter offers us a key mindset to think about. Kotter suggests that good leadership depends fundamentally on the ability to build relationships, for without these it is impossible to communicate vision and inspire others. From Rousseau we can conclude that all leaders work in partnership with their followers, and therefore negotiation and bargaining skills will be crucial to effectiveness. And from Laozi we can take the simple principle that sometimes less is more. Leaders do not have to be active all the time. Sometimes it is best to surrender control, step back and let others take over.

Forget the false authority of transformational leadership and the false humility of personal leadership; put both aside. The paradox of need and rejection tells us that true leadership is based on a complementarity of needs, skills and abilities. It requires both parties to assess honestly what they have, and seek partners who can provide what is missing, on a basis of equality, humility and confidence. People might not want to be led, but if this complementarity is provided they will accept leadership and work with leaders to get things done. Leadership, then, is not something you do *to* people, or *for* them; it is something you do *with* them.

Questions for reflection and discussion

1. How do you feel about being led? Do you agree with Jefferson that submission to others is 'the last degradation of a free and moral agent', or do you think leadership is a positive force? Do you yourself actually *like* being led? Think about this, and write a short 50 or 100 word note summarising your thoughts. Then reflect on this.
2. Having summarised your own view of leadership, how do you think the people whom you lead feel about being led? Do they really, genuinely, want you to lead them? Or do they accept your leadership as a perhaps unpleasant necessity? Or are their views somewhere between those positions? What does this mean for your own leadership style?
3. 'The highest type of ruler is one of whose existence the people are barely aware.' Could you lead like this? Could you trust the people you lead to do the right thing, without you there to guide them? If not, why not?
4. 'Each of us places his person and authority under the supreme direction of the general will, and the group receives each individual as an indivisible part of the whole.' How might this work in practice? How might each party understand their role in the social contract, and how would leadership have to change to accommodate this concept?
5. One implication from John Kotter's work is that people might want to be led, but they do not want to be managed. But can you be a successful leader without also knowing how to manage? Consider this, and discuss with your colleagues.

Recommended reading

Follett, Mary Parker (1937) 'The Process of Control', in Luther H. Gulick and Lyndall Urwick (eds), *Papers on the Science of Administration*, New York, NY: Institute for Public Administration, pp. 161–169.

Goffee, Rob and Jones, Gareth (2006) *Why Should Anyone Be Led by You?* Boston, MA: HBS Press.

Sidani, Yusuf M. (2008) 'Ibn Khaldun of North Africa: An AD 1377 Theory of Leadership', *Journal of Management History* 14(1): 73–86.

Whitehead, Thomas North (1936) *Leadership in a Free Society: A Study in Human Relations Based on an Analysis of Present-Day Industrial Civilization*, Oxford: Oxford University Press.

Witzel, Morgen (2012) *A History of Management Thought*, London: Routledge.

Witzel, Morgen (2014) *Management from the Masters*, London: Bloomsbury.

References

Adair, John (1989) *Not Bosses But Leaders*, Guildford: Talbot Adair Press.

Argyris, Chris (1957) *Personality and Organization*, New York, NY: Harper & Row.

Bennis, Warren (1989) *On Becoming a Leader*, Reading, MA: Addison-Wesley.

Bijapurkar, Rama (2008) *We Are Like That Only*, New Delhi: Penguin India.

Boyd, Steven R. (ed.) (1985) *The Whiskey Rebellion: Past and Present Perspectives*, Westport: Greenwood Press.

Burns, James McGregor (1978) *Leadership*, New York, NY: Harper & Row.

Carlin, Michael (2011) 'Employers are Watching Your Facebook', *National Law Review*, 6 June, available at: http://bit.ly/1WDCtCd.

Goffee, Rob and Jones, Gareth (2007) 'Leading Clever People', *Harvard Business Review*, March, available at: https://hbr.org/2007/03/leading-clever-people/ar/1.

Greenleaf, Robert K. (1977) *Servant Leadership*, Mahwah: Paulist Press.

Guardian (2012) 'Government Plans Increased Email and Social Network Surveillance', available at: www.theguardian.com/world/2012/apr/01/government-email-social-network-surveillance.

Guardian (2013) 'Google Chairman Eric Schmidt Defends Tax Avoidance Policies', available at: www.theguardian.com/technology/2013/apr/22/google-eric-schmidt-tax-avoidance.

Herzberg, Frederick (1966) *Work and the Nature of Man*, Cleveland: World Publishing Company.

Hofstede, Geert (1980) *Culture's Consequences: International Differences in Work-Related Values*, Beverly Hills: Sage.

Jefferson, Thomas (1989) Letter to Francis Hopkinson, 13 March 1789, full text available at: www.britannica.com/presidents/article-9116912.

Kets de Vries, Manfred (2004) *Lessons on Leadership by Terror: Finding Shaka Zulu in the Attic*, Cheltenham: Edward Elgar.

Kotter, John P. (1990) *A Force for Change: How Leadership Differs from Management*, New York, NY: The Free Press.

Lubman, Stanley (2014) 'Labor Pains: A Rising Threat to Stability in China', *Wall Street Journal*, 10 June, available at: http://blogs.wsj.com/chinarealtime/2014/06/10/labor-pains-a-rising-threat-to-stability-in-china/.

MacFarquhar, Roderick and Schoenhals, Michael (2006) *Mao's Last Revolution*, Cambridge, MA: Harvard University Press.

Maslow, Abraham (1954) *Motivation and Personality*, New York, NY: Harper & Bros.

Mayo, Elton (1933) *The Human Problems of an Industrial Civilization*, New York, NY: Macmillan.

Milkis, Sidney M. and Nelson, Michael (2008) *The American Presidency: Origins and Development*, Washington, DC: CQ Press.

Mintzberg, Henry (1973) *The Nature of Managerial Work*, New York, NY: Harper & Row.

Moore, Karl and Klein, Alexandra (2013) 'John Paul Kotter', in Morgen Witzel and Malcolm Warner (eds), *The Oxford Handbook of Management Thinkers*, Oxford: Oxford University Press, pp. 462–479.

Rasmussen Reports (2013) '63% View Too-Powerful Government As Bigger Threat Than Weaker One', available at: http://bit.ly/1NE5VSB.

Ross, Michael (1975) *Banners of the King: The Revolt in the Vendée, 1793*, New York, NY: Hippocrene Books.

Rousseau, Jean-Jacques (1998) *The Social Contract*, London: Wentworth.

Scribner, R.W. (1987) *Popular Movements and Popular Culture in Reformation Germany*, London: Continuum.

Semler, Ricardo (1993) *Maverick! The Success Story Behind the World's Most Unusual Workplace*, London: Arrow.

Thompson, Mark (2015) 'Political Power and a Hacking Scandal, Rupert Murdoch's Rise and Fall in Britain', available at: http://money.cnn.com/2015/06/11/media/murdoch-britain-media-empire/index.html.

Witzel, Morgen (2012) 'The Leadership Philosophy of Han Fei', *Asia Pacific Business Review*, pp. 489–503.

Witzel, Morgen (2013) 'Leaders and Managers Should be One and the Same', *Financial Times*, 3 June.

Wu, John C.H. (trans.) (1990) *Tao Teh Ching (Daodejing)*, London: Shambhala.

3

PARADOXES OF PERSPECTIVE

Leaders, leading and leadership

Richard Bolden

In this chapter Richard Bolden draws on his experience of studying leadership in a range of different contexts, including health care, higher education and international development, to highlight the limitations of traditional perspectives on leadership and to offer some alternatives. He explores concepts such as heroic, toxic, relational and distributed leadership and the different perspectives that each of these gives into the nature and processes of leadership in a complex and contested world. Through this analysis three paradoxes are identified that have significant implications for how we research, develop and recognise leadership in organisations and communities.

Introduction

Questions of leadership have been at the heart of business and society for thousands of years, yet the challenges of the new millennium have prompted substantial shifts in both the theory and practice of leadership that challenge traditional accounts of influence and agency.[1]

Concepts of distributed and shared leadership, for example, have become increasingly popular, as have approaches based on complexity science[2] and identity. Despite these developments the more we discover about leadership, the more elusive, ambiguous and contested it seems to become.

Leadership is a truly interdisciplinary subject and one that touches on many of the most important issues and questions of our times. This, of course, is what also makes it a frustrating and challenging topic of enquiry. Everyone has their own opinion on leadership and research insights are often partial, fleeting or ambiguous. As Meindl *et al.* (1985) observed, there is a romance to the concept of leadership that makes it difficult to pin down:

> It has become apparent that, after years of trying, we have been unable to generate an understanding of leadership that is both intellectually compelling and emotionally satisfying. The concept of leadership remains elusive and enigmatic.
>
> *(p. 78)*

Rather than being a problem to be solved, I suggest that engaging with the elusive and enigmatic qualities of leadership is key to understanding what it is and to enhancing leadership practice and its development. As Socrates famously proclaimed: 'the only true wisdom is in knowing you know nothing!'

In this chapter I use the concept of Paradox to highlight the limitations of traditional perspectives on leadership and to offer some alternatives. A paradox is defined as 'a statement or proposition that seems self-contradictory or absurd but in reality expresses a possible truth' or 'an opinion or statement contrary to commonly accepted opinion' (dictionary.com, 2015). It is different from the notion of a 'dilemma' or 'conundrum' in that it does not suggest the need to make a decision between two or more alternatives and nor does it suggest the possibility of finding a resolution.

A paradox requires us to accept that multiple truths may co-exist simultaneously – something that we in the West can struggle with. As the American theatre director Shellen Lubin noted:

> Living with contradiction may be nothing new to humans, but acknowledging it, and accepting it are. Even the dictionary has trouble accepting a paradox, calling it 'two things that seem to be contradictory but may possibly be true.' But that's not a real paradox – a real paradox IS contradictory and IS true.
>
> *(goodreads.com, 2015)*

In this chapter I will highlight three paradoxes that have been revealed through my own work and explore their implications for leadership theory, practice and development. In particular these paradoxes focus on the tensions between individual and shared perspectives on leadership.

The enduring allure of heroic leadership

A quick search on Google Images throws up lots of pictures where we see some figure, usually masculine in appearance, boldly showing the way whilst their faceless minions obediently follow. We're bombarded by these kinds of messages all the time, be it on television programmes such as *The Apprentice* or *Dragons' Den* – where young hopefuls desperately try to impress some authoritarian figure – or in the news – where our political leaders compete to be regarded as the most inspiring, authentic and dependable leader of the people.[3]

I have no doubt that, on reflection, most of us realise that such simplistic views of leadership are nonsense yet, in the Western world at least, they are hard-wired into us from an early age. I had the opportunity to test this out for myself a couple of years ago when I asked my children, then eight and six, two questions. The first of these was 'what is a leader?' and, almost immediately, my daughter piped up 'the person at the front of the line'. My second question, 'what is leadership?' was rather trickier and, after an uncomfortable moment's silence, my son suggested 'the ship at the front of the line'.

Such views, that suggest that leadership is all about leaders are referred to as leader-centric or 'heroic' approaches and they have a long history in both the scholarship and practice of leadership. The Scottish writer Thomas Carlyle (1840, p. 34) suggested: 'the history of the world is but the biography of great men'. This has become known as the 'Great Man Theory of Leadership' and despite extensive critique the idea has been difficult to dislodge.

In more recent years we have thankfully acknowledged the exceptional leadership of women as well as men. However, there remains a popular fascination with the personal stories of people who have achieved greatness . . . or increasingly it seems just some form of notoriety or celebrity.

There is no consistent scientific evidence, however, to suggest that leaders with particular traits or qualities are more likely to be successful than those with others, yet organisations of all kinds continue to develop and promote competency frameworks to measure and assess leadership capability.

A little over ten years ago my colleague Jonathan Gosling and I did some research to support the development of the National Occupational Standards in Leadership and Management[4] which underpin the National Vocational Qualifications Framework and which have subsequently been adopted by professional accreditation bodies such as the Chartered Management Institute.

In this work we compared the qualities identified in 30 of the most widely used leadership and management frameworks with characteristics identified as important to leadership and society by mid to senior leaders attending programmes at the Windsor Leadership Trust.[5] As you might expect, there were some significant areas of difference. Most notable was that, despite the importance attributed to them by the practising leaders, around two-thirds of the frameworks made no explicit reference to trust, ethics, inspiration, adaptability or resilience; and fewer than a fifth made reference to personal beliefs, courage, humility, reflection, work–life balance or an ability to cope with complexity (Bolden and Gosling, 2006).

Amongst the articles that we wrote based on this work was one entitled 'Is the NHS Leadership Qualities Framework missing the wood for the trees?' (Bolden *et al.*, 2006). In brief, the answer was 'yes' – in that we suggested the focus on measurable individual behaviours largely overlooked the inherently relational, emotional and ethical nature of leadership and management in a health care context.

By attempting to boil leadership down to its basic ingredients the NHS and the many other organisations whose frameworks we analysed were in danger of missing the point – leadership is not simply the sum of its parts! Much like concepts such as love, beauty and creativity, leadership has an aesthetic quality that cannot be sub-divided and which defies purely rational analysis.

This brings us to the first of the paradoxes:

> ***Paradox 1*** *– in attempting to identify and measure the essence of leadership we may inadvertently lose sight of the very thing we are seeking to capture.*

To draw parallels to biology, a focus on leadership traits and qualities is rather like trying to understand a rare species of bird by capturing, killing and dissecting it. There are certainly things to be learnt but all we're left with at the end of the day is a pile of feathers, bone and flesh and little opportunity for further enquiry. If, however, we seek to understand the bird's behaviour, appreciate its beauty or understand the part it plays in the wider ecosystem we need to take a somewhat different approach. We need to find ways to observe it in its natural surroundings – to watch it in flight, in interaction with other members of its species and to carefully study the environment in which it lives.

Towards a relational perspective on leadership

Recent years have seen increased calls for greater inclusion and participation in leadership and decision-making that shift the perspective from 'who' is leading to 'how' leadership is accomplished. This approach regards leadership as 'a social influence process through which emergent coordination (i.e. evolving social order) and change (i.e. new values, attitudes, approaches, behaviours, ideologies, etc.) are constructed and produced' (Uhl-Bien, 2006, p. 668) – no longer an attribute of individuals themselves but a property of the system . . . or paradoxically perhaps both.

My opportunity to explore the relational nature of leadership arose through a project I undertook for the British Council, along with my colleague Phil Kirk. This project took us to sub-Saharan Africa to explore and evaluate the process and impacts of a Pan-African leadership development programme called 'Interaction'. At the heart of this programme was the simple belief that anyone with some motivation and a willingness to engage in leadership could have an immense impact. The programme, delivered over a period of six months to a cohort of 300 participants from 19 African nations, sought to catalyse people's engagement with their communities both locally and more widely across the continent.

These remarkable people came from all walks of life. There were bankers, doctors, students, teachers, lawyers, administrators, and many more – each of whom had responded to an advert inviting them to apply if they were passionate about Africa and wanted to make a positive difference. The programme itself did little more than bring people together, to encourage them to embrace a few simple principles and to engage in dialogue. Much of the time on the programme involved them working with a local organisation – such as a children's home, a community project or a school – to help mobilise leadership amongst those they met.

I had the pleasure of both spending time with the participants and the communities they had visited and was struck by the way in which this initiative facilitated a shift in perspective from 'leaders' to 'leadership' – from the idea that leadership is something possessed by the few to leadership as a shared responsibility in which everyone has a part to play (Bolden and Kirk, 2006, 2009).

In analysing findings we used a systemic framework for leadership development and suggested that the programme gave participants the opportunity to walk, talk and see new possibilities for leadership together (Bolden and Kirk, 2011). It wasn't a case of learning complex theories and models or of developing specific skills or competencies – but rather of coming to recognise a sense of profound connection to others and the wider environment in which we are located; what theorists such as George Herbert Mead (1934) call the 'relational self'.

We concluded the paper by suggesting that: 'leadership is the mobilization of human effort in a collective enterprise' (2011, p. 33). This is not a romantic ideal, but an endeavour that is accomplished in the midst of contradictions, inequalities, conflicts, hopes and disappointments – as illustrated by the story of a Tanzanian grandmother's attempts to propagate and plant trees in the face of poverty and drought. When asked how it was that an elderly woman could undertake this feat she dismissed the question saying that if one was alive one could do it!

A concept that I discovered whilst in Africa, and which I've continued to explore ever since, is that of 'Ubuntu'. A Zulu word, with parallels in many other African languages, ubuntu is commonly translated into English with the phrase 'I am because we are'. It is best described as a philosophy of social interdependence, founded on principles of care and community, harmony and hospitality, respect and responsiveness. There is an associated saying that goes 'it takes a village to raise a child' which conveys a need for diversity and shared responsibility (Bolden, 2014).

In South Africa Ubuntu was a fundamental pillar of the Truth and Reconciliation Commission chaired by Archbishop Desmond Tutu in the late 1990s that sought to document, bear witness and on occasion grant pardon for the wrongdoings perpetrated under Apartheid. Tutu has called Ubuntu 'the gift that Africa will give the world' and, amongst others including Bill Clinton, has called for its wider adoption beyond Africa (see Mangaliso, 2001, Lutz, 2009).

Ubuntu and the concept of the relational self, described earlier, hold some interesting implications for the notions of heroic and individualistic leadership that continue to dominate thinking in most countries.

If, indeed, we are highly dependent on others for both our sense of who we are and what we can accomplish then the common distinction between 'leaders' and 'followers' may be unhelpful in that it creates a false dichotomy between the roles played by members of a group.

The dysfunctional effects of this way of thinking were highlighted in a seminal paper by Gemmill and Oakley (1992) where they described leadership as 'an alienating social myth' that 'functions as a social defence whose central aim is to repress uncomfortable needs, emotions and wishes that emerge when people work together' (p. 114). In idealising the leader, they argue, members detach themselves from their own visions and emotions and become complicit in maintaining the status quo.

We need only look at the banking industry over the past few years to get a sense of the importance of being able to challenge dysfunctional leadership (see Hutton, 2014, for a review), yet this is not easy. In the opening paragraph of her book titled *The Allure of Toxic Leaders* Jean Lipman-Blumen (2005) says:

> Toxic leaders cast their spell broadly. Most of us claim we abhor them. Yet we frequently follow – or at least tolerate – them, be they our employers, our CEOs, our senators, our clergy, or our teachers. When toxic leaders don't appear on their own, we often seek them out. On occasion, we even create them by pushing good leaders over the toxic line. That paradox of ambivalence ticks at the core of this book. Exploring that paradox, plus the strategies we might use to recognize, avoid,

> reform, overthrow, or escape from destructive and corrupt leaders, is the challenge of the *Allure of Toxic Leaders*.
>
> *(p. ix)*

As early as the 1940s Mary Parker Follett (1942/2003) argued for recognition of leadership as a reciprocal relationship between leaders and followers, and in 1954 the Australian psychologist C.A. Gibb suggested: 'leadership is probably best conceived as a group quality, as a set of functions which must be carried out by the group' (Gibb, 1954, p. 884).

It has, however, taken a long time for the rest of the world to catch up with them and it is only really since the turn of the millennium that concerted efforts have been made to develop and extend robust theory and research on shared and distributed leadership that put the collective and relational nature of leadership at their heart (see Bolden, 2011, for a review).

This then takes us to the second paradox:

> ***Paradox 2*** – *to better understand leadership we should spend less time studying 'leaders'.*

What I mean here is that, in organisations and other spheres of life, people carry roles and responsibilities that, to a certain degree, dictate the ways in which they will interact with others. A chief executive, for example, has a formal responsibility for the running of an organisation; a parent or teacher has different obligations from a child; yet none can accomplish outcomes alone and all operate within a set of norms and structures. They are also all subject to reciprocal influence, in that there are times when roles are flipped – for example when a child leads the parent or a staff member leads their manager.

We all experience this at some point but it's surprising how rarely it's acknowledged – that all leaders need to be able to follow and the best followers are those that can lead. Leading and following are two sides of the same coin and most of us are very skilled at switching between them – at taking turns as 'leader' and 'follower' and, on occasion, both or neither.

The American academic Joanne Ciulla (1998, p. 1) says that: 'leadership is not a person or a position. It is a complex moral relationship between people, based on trust, obligation, commitment, emotion, and a shared vision of the good.' And the British leadership scholar, Keith Grint, concludes:

> Leadership . . . is not just a theoretical arena but one with critical implications for us all and the limits of leadership – what leaders can do and what followers should allow them to do – are foundational aspects of this arena. Leadership, in effect, is too important to be left to leaders.
>
> *(Grint, 2005a, p. 4)*

Leadership as a distributed process

So if we need to broaden our perspective beyond 'leaders' where should we look and where do we draw the line between leadership, management and other processes?

One concept that I've found useful in addressing these questions is that of 'distributed leadership', which, according to Bennett *et al.* (2003, p. 7), suggests that:

1. 'leadership is an emergent property of a group or network of interacting individuals';
2. 'there is openness to the boundaries of leadership'; and
3. 'varieties of expertise are distributed across the many, not the few'.

Much of the original research on distributed leadership was done in the school sector and it is now firmly embedded in teacher training and development and even the regulatory framework of organisations such as Ofsted in the UK.

In my own work I've explored the application of these ideas to the higher education sector. Whilst studying leadership in your own sector can at times seem a little too close to home I've found universities to be a very interesting context in which to explore questions of leadership, influence and identity.

A cartoon that was published in the *Times Higher Education Supplement* alongside an article summarising the findings of a study we conducted on 'Developing collective leadership in higher education' (Bolden *et al.*, 2008) nicely captures some of the ambiguity around leadership in universities. It shows an alien who has landed on a university campus being told by an academic 'we don't have a leader to take you to'.

The idea that there is an absence of leadership in higher education and that leading academics is like herding cats of course speaks to popular stereotypes but is somewhat misleading. At the risk of spoiling the joke I'd like to suggest that the academic might go on to explain his response by saying 'because there are many leaders, contributing to different aspects of the academic enterprise, and who serve different functions for different communities'.

The idea that leadership takes many forms and that it is the combination of these influences that matters was brought home particularly strongly in a more recent study for the Leadership Foundation for Higher Education (Bolden *et al.*, 2012).

Whilst recent years have seen increasing emphasis and investment on leadership in universities most of this has focused on people with formal management responsibilities and has framed leadership in terms of organisational goals and objectives. Our project, however, explored the leadership of academic work from the perspective of those being led.

Through a combination of methods, we explored where and when academics look for leadership and found that, in most cases, the greatest influence comes from people who are not in formal authority relationships with them.

The word cloud in Figure 3.1 shows the descriptions our respondents gave when identifying people who exerted most influence over their academic work. Out of over 400 responses only one person made direct reference to anyone in the senior executive team of the university. This, of course, is not to say that they are unimportant but does highlight the significance of informal leadership, much of which comes from people outside the respondent's own department or institution.

In the interviews when we began asking about academic leadership in most cases people went to long lengths to explain that it is not 'academic management'. Findings suggested that academics across the sector tended to recognise leadership in actions that (a) provide and protect an environment that enables productive academic work, (b) support and develop a sense of shared academic values and identity,

FIGURE 3.1 Word cloud of most influential persons (Bolden *et al.*, 2012, p. 18).

Reproduced with the permission of the Leadership Foundation for Higher Education.

and (c) accomplish boundary spanning on behalf of individuals and work groups (Bolden *et al.*, 2012).

One of my favourite quotes from the interviews was from a lecturer who, when asked, 'who do you look to for leadership?' replied:

> People I've never met, mostly – some of them dead . . . And my supervisor of my doctorate degree as well . . . As a more mature academic, I've enjoyed working with collaborators. But that's not leadership. I really dislike this concept of leadership, because once you're grown up, you don't want to be led, you want to work as a member of a team.
>
> *(Bolden* et al.*, 2012, p. 30)*

This quote says quite a lot about leadership and followership in universities. Firstly that we choose our leaders, and that they may not necessarily be aware of their influence on us. Secondly, that there are times in our career, particularly when we are developing our professional practice, where people such as PhD supervisors and line managers can play a very important developmental leadership role (even if it is not often described as such). And thirdly, that much of the time we do not actually want to be led by someone else, but would rather be able to lead ourselves in relation to what the work requires.

Figure 3.2 shows a diagram we developed to try to capture the distinction between academic leadership, academic management and self-leadership that was being made by participants in this study.

We call it the 'sailing ship' model and it suggests that an effective environment for academic work requires a balance between 'academic leadership', which shapes values and identities, and 'academic management', which focuses on the allocation and completion of tasks and processes. Where these are aligned they create a coherent sense of academic purpose, goals and objectives that are then accomplished through 'self-leadership' by academic professionals.

Much as we liked the sailing ship model, however, we felt that it was rather too neat and too static to capture the sense of dissonance many people expressed about leadership and management in their own institutions. So we developed this second diagram – the 'sinking ship' (Figure 3.3).

This research was conducted in 2011 when English universities were negotiating a significant increase in student fees, preparing for the forthcoming national research assessment process and introducing changes to pensions and contracts. It was a time of substantial change and uncertainty about the purpose and future of UK higher education.

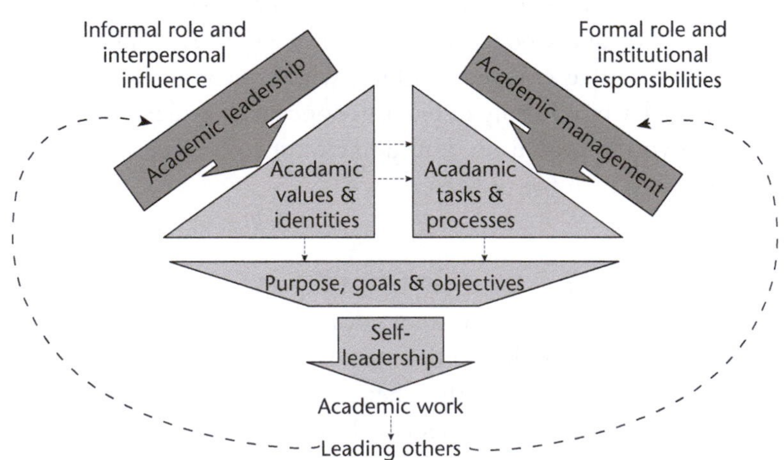

FIGURE 3.2 The 'sailing ship' model of academic leadership (Bolden *et al.*, 2012, p. 35).

Reproduced with the permission of the Leadership Foundation for Higher Education.

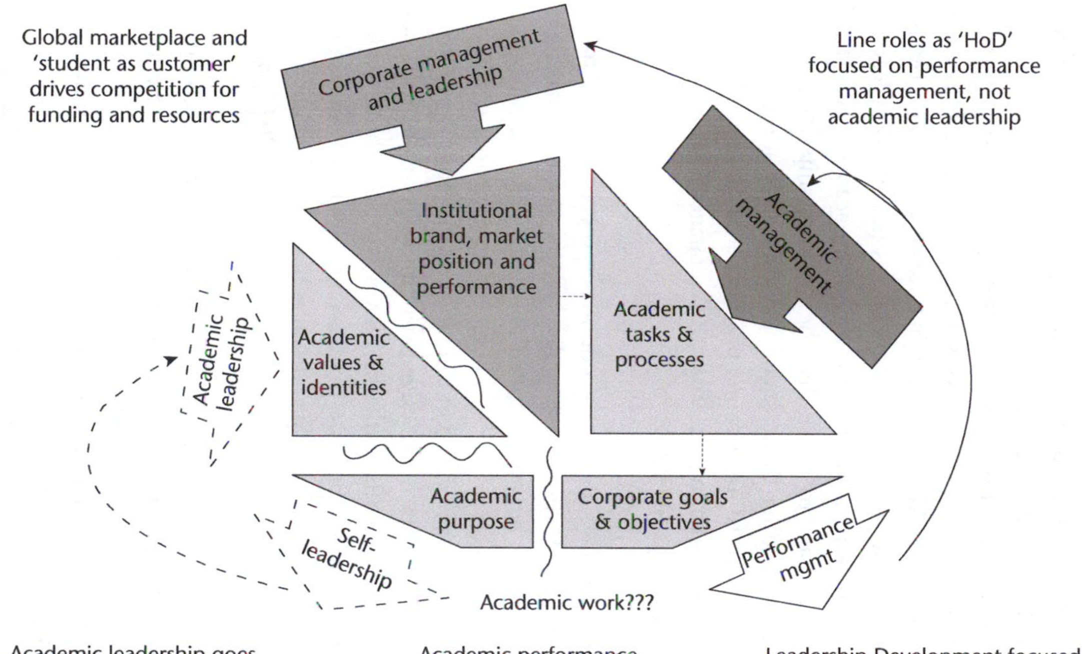

FIGURE 3.3 The 'sinking ship' model of academic leadership (Bolden *et al.*, 2012, p. 37).

Reproduced with the permission of the Leadership Foundation for Higher Education.

As you can see from Figure 3.3, there was a suggestion that competition for students and funding is driving a corporate leadership approach within institutions that is based on market principles and is implemented through formal management processes. In such a context, it was suggested 'academic leadership' might become fragmented, sidelined or go underground.

An example of this in our study was a junior lecturer in one university who campaigned to keep the university bookstore open following a campus redevelopment. Whilst this might be seen as resistance by the organisation itself, to academic colleagues it was perceived as leadership as it involved making a stand about important academic values.[6]

Whilst it is important to stress that the 'sinking ship' diagram is based on perceptions rather than objective reality it has some important implications for how institutions promote and facilitate leadership. In particular it highlights the risks of disengagement. As one of the participants in our study said:

> I think the tendency all over the country is to get more and more managerialist . . . I think, especially at universities, managers have to hold their nerve and trust their staff . . . looking around, I think most of us are engaged. There's a few who aren't, who've either burnt out or become extremely cynical, but I'd say most of us are engaged but we're engaged with the role and with our students, not necessarily with the university. So I think leaders have to work on that because there are times when I was almost alienated from the university and that is not a good thing.
>
> *(Bolden* et al., *2012, p. 33)*

Within our research we were frequently struck by a strong commitment to the ideals of higher education from our participants yet frequent ambivalence, and occasional hostility, towards their own employer.

The tension that such a situation can present for those who take on formal management and leadership roles is expressed well by the Critical Management scholar Martin Parker in his autobiographical paper titled 'Becoming manager: the werewolf looks anxiously in the mirror for signs of unusual facial hair', in which he describes his experience of taking on the role of head of department in a university where he had worked for some time.

The paper highlights the anxieties that arise when acquiring apparently conflicting roles and identities. Whilst it's perhaps inevitable that a person who has spent much of his professional life critiquing management will experience a degree of discomfort as he comes to terms with his new managerial role, the need to work through competing and sometimes contradictory identities is not unusual. Parker sums it up well when he says:

> I think that the most important distinction to be made is that I am a manager with an alternate 'professional' identity. Like other professionals in large organizations (doctors, engineers, lawyers) I have a somewhat divided series of identifications, some of which have little to do with my employer as such.
>
> *(Parker, 2004, p. 56)*

Despite the idiosyncrasies of the higher education sector we have found that our findings have resonated in a wide range of industries and well beyond the UK. With the rapid growth of professional and knowledge-intensive work rather than being an anomaly of higher education these issues are likely to become increasingly common across many sectors and occupations.[7]

This takes me to the third and final paradox:

> ***Paradox 3** – the most effective leadership is where 'leadership' is not required.*

In perhaps the first ever book on leadership, written in the fifth century BC, Lao Tzu, the founder of Daoism, said:

> A leader is best
> When people barely know he exists
> Not so good when people obey and acclaim him
> Worse when they despise him
> But of a good leader, who talks little,
> When his work is done, his aim fulfilled,
> They will say:
> We did it ourselves.
>
> *(Lao Tzu, cited in Manz and Sims, 1991, p. 35)*

It is ironic, therefore, that in most of our organisations it continues to be those who shout the loudest who tend to reap the greatest rewards and that most people's promotion opportunities depend on them highlighting how they, rather than others, achieved particular outcomes.

New leadership for new times

As I suggested at the start of this chapter, questions of leadership have long been of concern but it's really only been in the last 50–60 years that people have tried to systemically study and analyse leadership and only really in the last 20–25 years that a global leadership development industry has emerged.

Whilst this has undoubtedly contributed to our knowledge about leadership and the availability of leadership training and development I'm less convinced that it has had an equivalent impact on our understanding of leadership and, in particular, an understanding that will help us tackle the challenges we will face throughout the rest of this century.

Most of the leadership and management concepts and practices used in our organisations have their origins in an Industrial Era view of the world – where the centralisation of power and resources was important to support advances in manufacturing and production (Staron *et al.*, 2006).

In more recent years, particularly with the growth of computers and communications technology, we have moved towards a more networked view of organisations and alongside this we've seen a shift in emphasis from management and administration to leadership – from control to influence.

The changes since the turn of the millennium, however, have come at such a rate that it's been hard for both theory and practice to keep up. In reflecting on the changes that have happened since the publication of his book *The World is Flat* in 2005 Thomas Friedman noted:

> When I said the world is flat, Facebook didn't exist. Or for most people it didn't exist. Twitter was a sound. The Cloud was in the sky. 4G was a parking place. LinkedIn was a prison. Applications were something you sent to college. And, for most people, Skype was a typo. That all happened in the last seven

> years. And what it has done is taken the world from connected to hyper-connected. And that's been a huge opportunity and a huge challenge.
>
> *(Friedman, 2012)*

These, of course, are just the shifts in technology. In the past 15 years we've also seen the attack on the World Trade Center in New York and the subsequent War on Terror and rise of Islamic fundamentalism. We've come to recognise the extent of global climate change and the huge consequences this will have for future generations. We've had the global financial crisis and the subsequent austerity drive that continues to shape the geo-political landscape. We've seen an increase in the world population from six to over seven billion, of whom around 20 per cent now live in China. To paraphrase the Chinese proverb – we do indeed live in interesting times!

In the late 1990s the US Army War College developed the acronym 'VUCA' to refer to the volatile, uncertain, complex and ambiguous nature of the challenges facing nations in the post-Cold War era (Stiehm, 2010). In recent years the term has been applied to business, management and leadership (Johansen, 2009). Organisations in the public, private and third sector are increasingly recognising the challenges they face as 'wicked'[8] and in need of a collaborative response. In such situations the work of leadership is far less about providing answers than asking the right questions and ensuring the right people are engaged in developing a solution (Grint, 2005b, 2008).

In a VUCA world established approaches to strategy, planning and control often accentuate rather than alleviate the problem. Turbulent times highlight all too quickly the limits of traditional models of leadership and leadership development that focus almost exclusively on what is happening at the top of the organisation. Whilst the CEO, chairman and other members of the senior leadership team are clearly important, the factors that contribute towards organisational adaptability, innovation and performance are far more widely distributed. Context, both internal and external to the organisation, ultimately determines what works . . . but often in ways that could not have been anticipated in advance.

So to return to the notion of paradox – much as quantum physicists such as Paul Callaghan and Niels Bohr have embraced a science of uncertainty to rethink the nature of our physical world I believe that similar advances are required in our understanding of the social world.

There is, indeed, an emerging area of study within the field of leadership around the application of a complexity approach (Stacey, 2010; Obolensky, 2010; Uhl-Bien *et al.*, 2007) and a number of organisations that are championing this within the field of leadership development. Flinn and Mowles (2014) summarise the implications as follows:

> From the perspective of complex responsive processes of relating, leading leadership development involves encouraging radical doubt, enquiry and reflexivity as a way of developing the capacity of leaders to manage in circumstances of high uncertainty and ideological and political contestation. However, radical doubt does not mean throwing everything up in the air at once. It means learning how to navigate between the poles of absolute certainty and absolute doubt, while persisting in seeing the world as more complex than it is portrayed in the dominant discourse.
>
> *(p. 19)*

Conclusion

In this chapter I've suggested that there are a number of paradoxes that emerge when researching, practising and developing leadership. Many of these relate to the tensions between traditional perspectives, that tend to present leadership as an individual quality, competence or behaviour, and shared perspectives, that regard leadership as a reciprocal process of influence.

I suggest that in an interdependent and networked society an ability to embrace and work with paradox and complexity is a key part of effective leadership. Rather than providing direction, control and decision-making, leaders increasingly influence through sensemaking, boundary spanning and providing a compelling narrative. Leadership, however, is ultimately a group process and, as this chapter argues, we would do well to rethink the leader–follower relationship in order to find ways of mobilising the collective capacity of individuals, groups, organisations and communities.

Barker (1997, p. 352) describes leadership as 'a process of change where the ethics of individuals are integrated into the mores of a community'. From this perspective leadership development is an important forum for negotiating shared values and purpose and is ultimately a process of community development.

Questions for reflection and discussion

These questions can be explored individually, in pairs or in a small group.

1. How is leadership recognised, rewarded and developed in your work context? What are the effects (both intended and unintended) of this on individual and group behaviour?
2. What competing goals and priorities can you identify in your work? How do you and/or colleagues navigate between these tensions?
3. What kind(s) of challenge(s) do you face at work? To what extent are these linked to wider factors outside your control? How might taking a systemic perspective change the way you think about these issues and how to resolve them?
4. Identify three unsung heroes at work or in your community? How might their contribution be acknowledged in terms of leadership?
5. What are the key identities you carry at work, home and in the community? Are there any tensions/conflicts? How might it be possible to reframe these to give a broader, more inclusive sense of self?

Notes

1 The term 'agency' is used to express the degree of free choice a person has (or believes him/herself to have) when deciding how to act within a particular context/situation.

2 A complexity approach suggests that rather than viewing organisations as rational, bounded systems that can be managed in predictable and controlled ways, they are better conceived of as 'patterns of human interaction constantly emerging in both predictable and unpredictable ways in the living present, mostly through conversational activity' (Flinn and Mowles, 2014, p. 2).

3 See, for example, the BBC Election Debate 2015, http://tiny.cc/bbc-election-debate-2015.

4 www.management-standards.org/standards/standards.
5 The Windsor Leadership Trust describes itself as 'a charity that provides transformational leadership development programmes, for senior leaders from all sectors of society', www.windsorleadership.org.uk.
6 Some authors now refer to this as 'resistance leadership' (Zoller and Fairhurst, 2007).
7 Indeed, evidence suggests that a sense of autonomy, mastery and purpose are the strongest motivational drivers for people in all kinds of work and have a significant positive impact on health and wellbeing (Pink, 2009).
8 A 'wicked' problem is complex, intractable and cannot be resolved through the application of prior knowledge.

Recommended reading

Barker, R.A. (1997) How can we train leaders if we do not know what leadership is? *Human Relations* 50(4): 343–362.

Bolden, R. and Gosling, J. (2006) Leadership competencies: time to change the tune? *Leadership* 2(2): 147–163.

Bolden, R., Hawkins, B., Gosling, J. and Taylor, S. (2011) *Exploring Leadership: Individual, Organizational and Societal Perspectives*. Oxford: Oxford University Press.

Ghate, D., Lewis, J. and Welbourn, D. (2013) *Systems Leadership: Exceptional Leadership for Exceptional Times – Synthesis Paper*. Nottingham: Virtual Staff College.

Grint, K. (2008) Wicked problems and clumsy solutions: the role of leadership, *Clinical Leader* 1(2). Available at: http://bit.ly/1HqT8CH, accessed 1 November 2014.

References

Barker, R.A. (1997) How can we train leaders if we do not know what leadership is? *Human Relations* 50(4): 343–362.

Bennett, N., Wise, C., Woods, P.A. and Harvey, J.A. (2003) *Distributed Leadership*. Nottingham: National College of School Leadership.

Bolden, R. (2011) Distributed leadership in organizations: a review of theory and research, *International Journal of Management Reviews* 13(3): 251–269.

Bolden, R. (2014) Ubuntu, in David Coghlan and Mary Brydon-Miller (eds) *The SAGE Encyclopedia of Action Research*. London: Sage Publications, pp. 799–802.

Bolden, R. and Gosling, J. (2006) Leadership competencies: time to change the tune? *Leadership* 2(2): 147–163.

Bolden, R. and Kirk, P. (2006) From 'leaders' to 'leadership', *Effective Executive* 8(10): 27–33.

Bolden, R. and Kirk, P. (2009) African leadership: surfacing new understandings through leadership development, *International Journal of Cross Cultural Management* 9(1): 69–86.

Bolden, R. and Kirk, P. (2011) Leadership development as a catalyst for social change: lessons from a pan-African programme, in S. Turnbull, P. Case, G. Edwards, D. Schedlitzki and P. Simpson (eds) *Worldly Leadership: Alternative Wisdoms for a Complex World*. Basingstoke: Palgrave Macmillan, pp. 32–51.

Bolden, R., Petrov, G. and Gosling, J. (2008) *Developing Collective Leadership in Higher Education: Final Report*. London: Leadership Foundation for Higher Education.

Bolden, R. Wood, M. and Gosling, J. (2006) Is the NHS Leadership Qualities Framework missing the wood for the trees? in A. Casebeer, A. Harrison and A.L. Mark (eds) *Innovations in Health Care: A Reality Check*. New York, NY: Palgrave Macmillan, pp. 17–29.

Bolden, R., Gosling, J., O'Brien, A., Peters, K., Ryan, M. and Haslam, S.A. (2012) *Academic Leadership: Changing Conceptions, Identities and Experiences in UK Higher Education*. London: Leadership Foundation for Higher Education.

Carlyle, T. (1840) *On Heroes, Hero-Worship, and the Heroic in History*. London: Chapman and Hall.

Ciulla, J. (1998) *Ethics: The Heart of Leadership*. Westport, CT: Praeger.

Dictionary.com (2015) Paradox. Available at: http://dictionary.reference.com/browse/paradox, accessed 15 April 2015.

Flinn, K. and Mowles, C. (2014) A complexity approach to leadership development: developing practical judgement. LFHE Stimulus Paper. London: Leadership Foundation for Higher Education.

Follett, M.P. (1942/2003) *Dynamic Administration: The Collected Papers of Mary Parker Follett*. London: Routledge.

Friedman, T.L. (2005) *The World is Flat: A Brief History of the Globalized World in the Twenty-First Century*. London: Allen Lane.

Friedman, T.L. (2012) On 'connected to hyperconnected', *Huffington Post*, 28 September. Available at: http://huff.to/1CNx3HW, accessed 2 May 2015.

Gemmill, G. and Oakley, J. (1992) Leadership: an alienating social myth? *Human Relations* 45(2): 113–129.

Gibb, C.A. (1954) Leadership, in G. Lindzey (ed.) *Handbook of Social Psychology*, Vol. 2. Reading, MA: Addison-Wesley, pp. 877–917.

Goodreads.com (2015) Shellen Lubin: quotes. Available at: http://bit.ly/1FdGfbd, accessed 5 March 2015.

Grint, K. (2005a) *Leadership: Limits and Possibilities*. Basingstoke: Palgrave Macmillan.

Grint, K. (2005b) Problems, problems, problems: the social construction of 'leadership', *Human Relations* 58(11): 1467–1494.

Grint, K. (2008) Wicked problems and clumsy solutions: the role of leadership, *Clinical Leader* 1(2). Available at: http://bit.ly/1HqT8CH, accessed 1 November 2014.

Hutton, W. (2014) Banking is changing, slowly, but its culture is still corrupt, *Guardian*, 16 November. Available at: http://tiny.cc/hutton-banking, accessed 14 March 2015.

Johansen, B. (2009) *Leaders Make the Future*. San Francisco, CA: Berrett-Koehler.

Lipman-Blumen, J. (2005) *The Allure of Toxic Leaders*. New York, NY: Oxford University Press.

Lutz, D.W. (2009) African ubuntu philosophy and global management, *Journal of Business Ethics* 84: 313–328.

Mangaliso, M.P. (2001) Building competitive advantage from Ubuntu: management lessons from South Africa, *Academy of Management Executive* 15(3): 23–33.

Manz, C.C. and Sims, H.P. (1991) Superleadership: beyond the myth of heroic leadership, *Organizational Dynamics* (Spring): 18–35.

Mead, G.H. (1934) *Mind, Self, and Society: From the Standpoint of a Social Behaviorist*. Chicago, IL: University of Chicago Press.

Meindl, J.R., Ehrlich, S.B. and Dukerich, J.M. (1985) The romance of leadership, *Administrative Science Quarterly* 30(1): 78–102.

Obolensky, N. (2010) *Complex Adaptive Leadership: Embracing Paradox and Uncertainty*. Farnham: Gower.

Parker, M. (2004) Becoming manager or, the werewolf looks anxiously in the mirror, checking for unusual facial hair, *Management Learning* 35: 45–59.

Pink, D.H. (2009) *Drive: The Surprising Truth About What Motivates Us*. New York, NY: Penguin-Riverhead.

Stacey, R.D. (2010) *Complexity and Organizational Reality*, 2nd edn. London: Routledge.

Staron, M., Jasinski, M. and Weatherley, R. (2006) *Life Based Learning: A Strength Based Approach for Capability Development in Vocational and Technical Education*. Darlinghurst, NSW: TAFE NSW International Centre for VET.

Stiehm, J.H. (2010) *U.S. Army War College: Military Education in a Democracy*. Philadelphia, PA: Temple University Press.

Uhl-Bien, M. (2006) Relational leadership theory: exploring the social processes of leadership and organizing, *The Leadership Quarterly* 17: 654–676.

Uhl-Bien, M., Marion, R. and McKelvey, B. (2007) Complexity leadership theory: shifting leadership from the industrial age to the knowledge era, *The Leadership Quarterly* 18(4): 298–318.

Zoller, H. and Fairhurst, G. (2007) Resistance leadership: the overlooked potential in critical organization and leadership studies, *Human Relations* 60(9): 1331–1360.

4

LEADERSHIP PARADOXES OF TEAM AND TIME

Nigel Linacre

In this chapter, Nigel Linacre places leadership in time and space, and explores the paradoxes that are inevitably present as soon as this is done. Leaders are like everyone else operating in the present, but they also have a sense of where the team is heading. A leader is within and beyond the team they lead, and a member of other teams. Having worked with leaders and would-be leaders in many countries via leadership coaching and workshops, his interest is in developing team and leadership capability, and he aims to create spaces in which you will find your own insights. You are encouraged to find your own answers as you read this work.

Leaders lead themselves and they lead teams and they may do both simultaneously. They attend to the circumstances of the present moment while intending a different future, and must be mindful of both. In this chapter we will explore the paradox inherent in leading both oneself and others, and then review the paradox of being present to this moment while focusing on the future, from a leadership perspective. Finally, we will consider both of the paradoxes together.

In doing so we will consider when a leader is *a part* of the group they lead or *apart* from it, and what would enable a leader to be accepted as part of the group even if their status tends towards separation, and how each may depend on the other. We'll also consider the need for being

TABLE 4.1 Paradoxes of team and time

	Being in the Present		Connecting with the Future
Leading Team	**Q3 Present Team**	*Team*	**Q4 Future Team**
	Present	*and/or*	*Future*
Leading Self	**Q1 Present Self**	*Self*	**Q2 Future Self**

present in the moment and in imaginatively anticipating the future. To start with, we can think of these in a matrix (see Table 4.1).

Horizontally we see the present on the left and the future on the right, while vertically we see the self, the team and the world that they together affect. Let's see if we can bring this simple construction to life by building some awareness of the four quadrants, beginning with a simple question of what are you aware of right now: these words and the physical book or electronic device on which you are reading them, the surrounding room or space in which you are now sitting or standing, the air that is coming into and going out of your body? Within that external or physical context you may also be aware of your thoughts about the experience that you are having now – 'What is this about, where is it going, does this make any sense, and how can I use it?' etc. – which we can think of as your internal or mental experience of this moment.

In most moments, you may have an imperfect or incomplete awareness of what is going on for yourself: if you start to notice your heartbeat in this moment you can be aware that in the previous moment you were unaware of your heart beating. The practice of 'self-awareness' (Duval and Wicklund, 1972), in which we have just been engaging, is a cornerstone of Emotional Intelligence (Goleman, 1996). However, while it is codified in Emotional Intelligence, self-awareness has been a cornerstone of different spiritual traditions for thousands of years, e.g. the *Bhagavad Gita*. It is also a core practice in much modern coaching.

As well as being aware of some aspects of yourself, you will have some 'awareness of others', including those who lead you and those whom you lead. When you were with someone recently, you may have noticed aspects of their physicality: face, hair, body, and so on, and you may also have had a sense of their general attitude and how they were feeling, which may or may not have matched their own sense. You may have had a clearer sense of their external appearance than their internal experience. Awareness of others, another cornerstone of Emotional Intelligence, is likely to be imperfect too. As a leader, you are bound to connect with others, both one-to-one and in groups or teams.

Think of a team of which you have been in: what was the team like, what did it feel like to be part of the team, what did you bring to the team and what did you receive from it? As well as awareness of (single) others, expressed in the concept 'awareness of others', we can think about 'team awareness'. Having laid a foundation of self-awareness, and expanded awareness of others, much of the work that I do with teams is about team awareness.

So far we've started to explore the self and others in the present moment, Quadrants 1 and 3 in Table 4.1. But we must also look to the future. If we are going to set off on a journey, it may be helpful to have some sense of where we are, and we must also want to have a sense of where we are going. If I ask you to follow me without giving you a sense of where we are going, you may be reluctant to follow my lead. We argue that leaders are continually in the business of co-creating the future (Linacre and Cann, 2011).

Let's consider your 'future self', but let's start with a question about the past: how are you different from the way you were, say, ten years ago, in what respects are you more aware, do you have more understanding, and perhaps more knowledge? If you can notice some progress in the past decade, you might reasonably hope for more progress in the next one. What progress would you like to make? Within organisations, we talk of realising human potential, the supposition being that there are as yet unrealised abilities, and we tend to assume that human development is always possible. This future-self practice is widespread. An Oscar-winning actor's acceptance speech shows his relentless focus on his future self, always five years out, always his hero (McConaughey, 2014). What would you like your future self to look like, to be like, and to accomplish? This may be your key question.

However much leaders may recognise their own responsibility to develop themselves, their responsibilities do not stop there. They also have a measure of responsibility not merely for their team's current performance but also for its development. Think of a team you have led or been in: how did it perform, where was it above average, where was it below average, what would an outstanding performance have looked like, what needed to shift within the team to get there? Going further, what would your ideal team have looked like, what would it have felt like to be in that team, and what key qualities would be present? One way or another, quickly or slowly, you can gain a sense of what a great team would look like, which provides some sense of the journey that you may wish to undertake, and on which you may persuade your colleagues to follow.

If you have not already done so, please explore your answers to the questions we have been asking so far. They will be unique. In all our leadership development work, we find participants gain the most when they discover their own answers.

Leadership turns out to be personal. Now that we have started to explore the self and others in the present moment and in terms of future possibilities, we can start to explore their paradoxical relationship to one another.

The one and the many

Everything a leader accomplishes is done through the vehicle of the leader him- or herself. The way a leader is being any time may make a difference to the team. A nervous leader is likely to put a team on edge. A calm, clear, present leader will also have an influence on the team.

On the other hand, a leader accomplishes everything through their team. A leader without a team is like a cox without oarsmen and women. She could call out 'stroke' but the boat is going nowhere. A leader accomplishes nothing without others.

Of course, a clean distinction between leaders and followers seldom describes the reality. We are all sometimes leading and sometimes following, and this changes from role to role, but it can also change from moment to moment. I'm co-founder of three organisations. In each organisation there are a total of two or three co-founders and there is no single leader and no hierarchy amongst us. In each moment I may be leading or following, or some mix of the two. We report to each other on the basis of equality and no one of us is in charge: we all are. At any moment in time any one of us is free to start leading. Once others respond, are we co-leading or following? Moment to moment it is hard to tell. In principle, leadership is a collective endeavour, in practice it can coalesce anywhere.

Something similar applies with our clients: an idea starts somewhere, it is developed somewhere else, and a potentially different team leads the implementation. If you've played for or follow a sports team: who is leading moment to moment in defence, midfield and attack? If I pass to you and then run forward, you may return the pass to me or see a more effective option. Was each of us leading in each moment that we had the ball? If so, leadership is constantly changing.

Think of your current roles: when are you leading, when are you following, can you identify moments in which you switch from leading to following and vice versa, is it obvious moment to moment who is leading or are there moments where it isn't clear who is leading?

However, in many organisations hierarchy is alive and well. Many years ago, when I was first promoted to the board of a small advertising agency I approached an account manager and said, 'Now I'm on the board I won't know what's really happening in the agency, so would you keep me posted?'. Even as a 30 year old it was clear to me that different levels of the organisation operated within their own bubbles and had radically different views of the same firm. There were things that you would be pleased to tell a board member and there would be other things that you would not dare to say. For example, I would be very happy to boast of the good work I had done to a board member but not any errors on my part, and I would provide only positive feedback to other board members. As is common in organisations where bad news is unwelcome, only good news would filter upwards. In joining the board I was crossing the Rubicon into what we may call 'Boardland'.

While we continued to work well, and I've described many good processes elsewhere (Linacre, 1987), the truth we clung to in Boardland was that we were definitely doing a good job, anything else was undiscussable (Argyris, 1990), and even when we began to realise that we could do better, it remained undiscussable. I was leading a team the members of which were not board members, and we had some successes, but my identity came from being a board member. That was my tribe.

At that stage in my development, I saw myself as above my team members, and when I was subsequently hired as managing director of a rival agency, this view became more marked. It was clear to me that I was good at my work, that after all was why I had been promoted, and I failed to see, let alone nurture, the talents of most of my colleagues. In terms of Transactional Analysis, I had gone into Parent mode, inviting other team members to take the role of Children (Berne, 1964). This may be a simplified view of what happened, but it is true nonetheless. Well, you can imagine what happened. After some initial success, the agency started to fail and was sold.

Is a leader *a part* of the group they lead or *apart* from the group? In this case, I had separated myself from the group I was leading. When you are leading a team, do you feel part of the team, or separate from the team? Do you try to get close to team members or keep some professional distance between you? If you have had more than one experience, how do your experiences vary? Did you sometimes feel part of the team you were leading, or the team in which you were one of a number of people reporting to a common boss?

Hierarchy remains hard-wired: in most organisations, appointments are top-down. Board members appoint senior managers each of whom appoint middle managers and so on. In most organisations people don't get to choose their leaders. Outside of elective politics, we've rarely tried making appointments the other way up. For better or worse, those who are supposed to lead are imposed on their teams. While a leader may inherit a team he or she is likely to replace some of the team members, shaping the new team in their image.

The leader's ability to hire and fire, promote and demote, may be constrained to some extent by due process, but even without being discussed let alone exercised, the power relationship is known and understood by both parties; it cannot be unknown. Titles communicate hierarchy too. Teams have 'Team Leaders', who report to Managers, who at some level report to a Chief. We started with Chief Executive Officers, and a growing number of organisations have a Chief Operating Officer, a Chief Financial Officer, a Chief Technology Officer and a Chief Marketing Officer, and more, so we now have the C-level. This speaks to where power is formally held, with the Chiefs. The Adult-to-Adult, as opposed to Parent–Child relationships, we may prefer, run against the organisational grain.

Speed and complexity

However, in the knowledge economy most modern organisations are complex. Consider an organisation in which you have worked: did you know everything that was happening in the organisation, did you know all that was happening even in one department, and for that matter did you know everything that was happening for a single colleague? These days it seems that no one knows everything, not even the team leader. Knowledge is everywhere but is nowhere in particular. If knowledge is power, then power is dispersed.

In fast-changing markets, organisations need to be fast-moving, which requires quick decision-making, so leadership has to be distributed. Each leader may set an overall set of objectives within which the leaders who report to them may set their objectives, and so on, what we could call a leadership cascade.

Within a team, leadership may not be limited to the team leader. We may hope many team members are capable of showing leadership when it's needed. Within an organisation where there are Chiefs at one level and Team Leaders at another, leadership cannot be limited merely to the Chiefs, since Team Leaders must also lead. We could say that we are all leaders now.

Leadership is to some extent distributed. You may have experienced this in practice. Think back to a time when you were in a high-performance team, the best team in which you have ever worked: who was leading, was it all about one individual or were there leadership contributions right across the team? As likely as not, leadership was a multi-person phenomenon. Effective leaders enable others to lead.

Still, leaders may want to be liked or at least appreciated by their colleagues. While leaders may be saddened when it does not seem to be practical, they may want to be friends with the people who report to them. Sometimes they have been promoted from within, and the people who now report to them were previously their peers, and may have been good friends or rivals or both.

In practice, none of these leaders is able to exercise power without the likelihood of significant consequences for themselves. To that extent, they are not laws unto themselves. All titular leaders rely on their team members to deliver the performance that is expected, they cannot do it alone, and without that performance their own positions are likely to be in jeopardy. Sooner or later the leader of an underperforming team will come under pressure.

Leaders can, on behalf of their organisations, demand a level of competence. But leadership performance is harder to measure in many situations than it used to be. You can measure outputs, but how much of that had to do with the circumstances, with a performance the team would have made anyway, and how much was due to an individual leader, may be hard to tell. Leaders can ask for a greater level of performance but cannot insist upon more than the bare requirement. From a people point of view, the key to high-performance in most organisations is the discretionary effort team members can provide (Haslam, 2004). As this effort is discretionary, team members may or may not provide it. You can ask for but not demand a great performance. To this extent, leaders are in thrall to their team members. While organisational structures go to some lengths to underline a hierarchy, the ability to choose to provide or withhold discretionary effort means the leader depends on the team. Which is another way of saying that it looks like the leader is in charge but it's the team.

Team members may not collectively decide to withhold discretionary effort: not in the official way trade unions have sometimes invited their members to go on a 'go-slow' or 'work-to-rule', meaning they would only do what the rules required. Team members may go to great efforts to make it look as though they are 'trying hard', and indeed may believe that they are, but without leadership that they appreciate they will not take as much trouble as their leaders would have wanted. In short, their hearts won't be in it. Outstanding results are then most unlikely.

The temptation of a leader who isn't getting great results is to blame the team. However, declining responsibility is itself a sign of poor leadership. If you want to find a good leader, you might start by finding a good team. That is evidence that, at the very least, the leader has not prevented the team from being or becoming a good team. If you find an individual who is not performing it may be down to them, but if you find a team that is not performing this suggests a failure of leadership. The relationship is symbiotic.

Unfortunately in some hierarchies executives put more energy into managing upwards than managing downwards, in trying to look good in the eyes of their boss. Where the hierarchy permits they may spend time challenging and reframing, but this is not always the case. Where challenge is discouraged, they may not challenge plans, even when they can see that they are unlikely to work. How can they be blamed for not seeing what their boss did not see? But as we suggested earlier, leaders with many reports cannot see all of the detail of each situation. In these conditions, the leaders become distanced from much of what is really happening within the organisation.

We have worked with organisations where the people at the top of the organisation continually maintain that things are going well even when they aren't. Those reporting to them go along with the view and feel unable to challenge upwards. They subscribe to the view that all is going well, and even protect the top level from evidence to the contrary. Now the top level is cut off from what is really happening within the organisation. The myth that all is going well is protected, even as evidence to the contrary emerges. Like Pangloss in *Candide*, they maintain that this is the best of all organisations (Voltaire, 1759).

Of course this is deeply damaging, because the leaders cannot address problems of which they are unaware. When problems finally do emerge, for example through a loss, those reporting to the top level leaders feel bound to reassure them that they can fix the problems, whether or not they can.

While this style of management has been sharply criticised, we may not place responsibility exclusively with those who are concealing the bad news. If senior management shoots a messenger who brings bad news, senior management has cut itself off.

Once the senior management has cut itself off from the flow of negative news, it no longer knows what isn't working, and is unable to identify problems, let alone analyse them or generate solutions. It may find it is working on the wrong problems or on no problems at all. Now the senior leaders aren't able to lead the organisation from where it really is. If you want to travel to Berlin and believe you are in Paris but you are actually in Moscow, heading east won't get you where you want to go. It may be helpful to have an upbeat view of where you want to go, but it may be vital to know where you are.

What do team members want from a leader, or from a performance perspective, what do team members require of a leader before they will perform? Do they want team leaders who are apart from the team or who are part of it? The question has only to be asked for the answer to be obvious, or at least part of the answer. Team members prefer leaders who engage with them (Buckingham and Coffman, 1999), except when a leader's inputs are considered unhelpful. Then, the further away the leader is the better. But this is unlikely where a leader has really engaged with the team.

Team members will want leaders to provide direction when it's needed, and who will take appropriate action when, for example, a team member is underperforming and undermining the team as a whole. Team members who are performing well rarely want a leader to be soft on poor performance, unless there is a good reason for it. In other words, team members may want to have it both ways. They want the leader to engage closely with them as though they are equals and they want the leader to stand back and provide leadership when it is called for and cannot so easily be provided by the rest of the team (Alimo-Metcalfe and Alban-Metcalfe, 2005).

All other things being equal, today's team members seek equal relationships, even when it may not be justified on the basis of experience, and this preference may be particularly pronounced amongst the millennials (Eden, 2013). This could be characterised as a preference for 'adult-to-adult' relationships as described in Transactional Analysis (Berne, 1964). Berne proposed that a party enters any transaction with another human being from a position of parent, adult or child. Someone who takes the parent role is inviting the other party to go into the child role, and vice versa, while someone who stays in the adult role is inviting the other party to be in the adult role too, forming an adult-to-adult relationship. Parent-to-child and adult-to-adult are both possible relationships, and are the most common. When one party takes the dominant parent position the other party does not have to take the child position, they could stay in the adult role, in which case there is a stand-off; one party or the other is likely to shift. While working in a team, we may hope that our ideas would be considered on merit, irrespective of our position in the hierarchy, in other words in an adult-to-adult way. In the old feudal model the King was in charge of the Lords who were in charge of the Knights and so on. He or she, and of course it was usually a he, called the shots and the team had to deliver. As we have already seen, work has shifted from manual labour towards creative problem-solving, performance can no longer be demanded, or even so easily measured, in the same way. When a team doesn't perform the team's nominal leader may imagine it is the team's responsibility or more usefully they may take responsibility themselves. Outstanding leaders may be quick to praise the team when things go well but take responsibility themselves when things don't go so well (Collins, 2001).

Working with leaders in workshops in Europe, America and Asia, we find that executives often feel underappreciated, and continue to have a hunger for more engagement. And as others have researched (Buckingham, 1999), greater engagement tends to lead to greater performance. But you may rely on your own experience when you ask yourself the question: what do you want from a leader?

We suggest that most people want their work to be appreciated, to be treated fairly and to sense that their work is contributing to something worthwhile. Haslam goes further and encourages leaders to embody the group. In his three Rs of social identity, leaders 'Reflect' the group, 'Represent' them, and enable them to 'Realise' their objectives (Haslam, 2010). Each team member can accomplish their goals while contributing to the goals of the organisation as a whole.

Good leaders encourage others to lead. If we consider the inclination to speak out when something needs to be said, to encourage when encouragement is needed, and so on, then why wouldn't a leader want to see at least a sprinkling of leadership throughout the team?

A leader must connect with colleagues and yet be able to disconnect. How can this paradox be resolved? Perhaps through the idea of connecting to something that is beyond both the leader and team, a common purpose which each of them serve (George, 2007). Then it is not about the leader or the team, it's about a common purpose. If we are involved in a power struggle, life may be very difficult, but if we are both attempting to realise a common goal, then we may transcend any disputes we would otherwise have encountered.

A leader who is only interested in the leader's welfare may be of little use to the team. A team that is only interested in its welfare may be of little use to the stakeholders it is supposed to serve. But a leader and team who are intent on accomplishing something beyond the leader and team, may be useful indeed. They both become servants of something more important.

This takes us on to the question of the present and the future for it is through time something more important may be accomplished.

The present and the future

Does a leader focus on the present or on the future, or on the path between one and the other? If they must do both how can they be reconciled? What does it mean to focus on the present and what does it mean to focus on the future? When is it relevant to focus on the present and how might one do so? When is it relevant to focus on the future and how might one do so? How might leaders become cut off from the present or for that matter lose sight of the future, and how might they reconnect with either?

Time waits for no man. Leaders work through time without which nothing can be accomplished. What is it that they do in time? Leaders transform: 'trans', to move across, from one 'form' to another. They may enable transformation for themselves, for the team they lead, and for the causes they serve; ideally, all three. One way and another, leadership and time are intimately connected. Intentionally or unintentionally, leaders enable the replacement of a form that life is taking with another form.

It's easy to be seduced by the present, but change is ever-present.

There must be a journey from the present into a future, but it is an unknown future. Come to that, it is an unknown journey. While those of a conservative position may resist, leaders are less often in the business of defending the present, particularly in the world of business. The leader's primary task is to enable the replacement of the present with something better. Leaders usher in the future (Johansen, 2012).

Let's take some examples: a leader is appointed to a new position, and charged with, say, growing the business, or turning around a division, or taking the organisation to the next level. In each case a transformation is required, and this is typically the case. Even where a leader is expected to preserve the heritage of a successful predecessor, circumstances change; and as the environment changes the organisation must also change, so standing still won't stand. Trying to be the previous leader rarely works.

It is often said that we are living in an age of ever-increasing change. In what respects might this be true? Let's think about this in terms of the Political, Economic, Social and Technological change factors, or the 'PEST' model (Aguilar, 1967). Technology is transforming industry after industry, and shows no sign of letting up. Technology has enabled the development of social media, which are driving some social change. Social change has been with us for some time. For those of us living in the Western world political change has been gradual for a generation, although this may change. A large fall in the values of shares listed on a stock market or the contraction of an economy by a percentage point or two for two consecutive quarters may seem to be a drama. In some parts of the world, including North Africa and the Middle East, there continue to be dramatic convulsions.

Within what we may still call the West there has recently been less drama, though the media continues to provide much excitement, most of which is from further afield. However, there is a gradual and unrelenting change, and organisations are expected to move forward every year, growing, becoming more efficient, and achieving better results every year.

Technological change powers most of today's economic change, which in turn influences social change, which influences the form that political change takes. Though politics can appear to be a slightly detached force of its own; sometimes loud, sometimes mute. Technology brings changes that are hard to predict, so that the change we embark on today may be overtaken by the time it is implemented. Leaders are leading us into the unknown (Grint, 2008).

While change may be more incremental than we might anticipate, the pressure is on to come up with the big idea, the big breakthrough that will be the game-changer, or at least find that breakthrough within the organisation. At this stage we might note that titular leaders rarely originate any such thing themselves. But they may create an environment in which others do so, or prompt the thousand little things that add up to a big difference.

Temporal leaders must have some sense of where their team or organisation could go. They are likely to draw upon their previous experience of what has worked in other places and in other times, and so approach the present through their lens of the past. But of course every situation is different.

In this context, let's more deeply explore the present and the future. What does it mean to be present or to be *in* the present? You may be familiar with the idea that ice cream never tastes so good the second time around. The first time we taste it, it's like 'wow', but the second time there's a little less wow. That may be because on subsequent occasions we are remembering what ice cream has tasted like and discounting the new when it more or less matches that memory. When there's a match there's no surprise. All we are doing is referencing the past. If we were really present, perhaps we could have had an equally big wow.

When we are looking through the selective lens of the past then we may not really see what the present has to offer, if we are thinking about something else then we may be distracted from the present; not really here. We could taste the present instead of referencing the past; we could be here now (Dass, 1971).

Leaders may base their understanding of the present on the reporting of the recent past. Senior leaders face a problem when others habitually misinform them. They may tell them what they think the senior leaders want to hear or what they think will serve their own purposes, and these often amount to the same thing. The common lie is that things are working, or that they are about to start working, even when the former may not be true and the second be improbable. The future is often varnished, and that may be expected, but rose-tinting the present may be equally commonplace.

Of course, a board may have a reasonably good picture of the current financial situation. Directors must be aware of cash, creditors and debtors, and of the ability of the organisation to go on trading. Beyond the financial information, what information do they really have? Each party reporting to the board may have an interest in looking as good as possible, in under-reporting difficulties and embossing achievements. This is less often about what has happened – a matter of fact – and more often a view of what is likely to happen in future: it's been a difficult year but we are well-placed for the future.

Winston Churchill described success as 'The ability to go from one failure to another with no loss of enthusiasm', or if you like no loss of nerve. It takes a strong leader to receive 'bad' news as equably as 'good', which brings to mind the poem 'If' (Kipling, 1910). In many organisations an unwanted truth prompts a bullet. Messengers are still getting shot.

Within an organisational context, connecting with the present is much more difficult, one might say occasional, than one might expect. And yet we would say it is fundamental. If you do not know where you are, how can you move on from there? If you do not know what is working and what is not, how can you fix what is not working? If you do not know your weaknesses, what will you do about them?

If the present is at one end of the bridge the future is at the other. How do you get into the future? Albert Einstein argued that 'Your imagination is your preview of life's forthcoming attractions'. We could observe that everything we see, the content of this book, its production, whatever clothes you are wearing, your job, your home, everything was imagined first. An unimagined future is, well, unimaginable.

You can imagine tomorrow, next month, next year, most of us do. This is not to be confused with the idea that all we need do is imagine things and they will miraculously manifest without any effort. It's just that without imagination we are flying blind, and probably flying nowhere. With the benefit of a clear vision, our unconscious knows where we want to go. As each event potentially moves us off course our vision brings us back again.

There's another way. It has been proposed that while mediocre organisations focus on 'how' and good organisations focus on 'what', great organisations focus on 'why' (Sinek, 2009). While *what* is static and *how* is limited, *why* is more likely to take us away from the present and into the future. In Latin languages, why is literally 'for-what'. If you embark on an activity without knowing your purpose, you are likely to lose your way. An incoming team leader could address the question: what is this team here for, what purpose is it supposed to fulfil? Consider a team you lead: what is its purpose? If you like, just start writing, *'The purpose of this team is to . . . '* An incoming organisational leader could ask: what is the purpose of this organisation? We are all invited to 'think outside the box': the box is *what*, *why* can get us outside of it.

It may be self-evident that a leader without a purpose is pointless, a team without a purpose is likely to drift and an organisation without a purpose would be pointless too. Some of us may have aimed to get to a particular position without having an idea of what we would be once we get there. We got the job: what then? Many corporate leaders have dodged the question of organisational purpose by saying that their goal is profit. Profit is the entry ticket. It provides sustainability, but sustainable for what?

It may be obvious, but it is only once we understand the purpose of the team, department or organisation, that we can sense how well it is accomplishing that purpose, let alone how the purpose may be more fully or effectively achieved. Purpose provides the bridge into the future.

With clarity about the purpose all involved can more easily start to envision something that is both relevant and different. The change may be incremental or radical, it may be made possible by changes in technology, it may be a response to a competitor, or be forced by a realisation that the organisation cannot go on as it is. Of course, many organisations resist change, and it is usually those that resist it the most that need it the most, but a sense of purpose can make a transition less difficult.

What has to change to get there? Before setting off on a journey it's a major advantage to have a sense of where you are going: 'Follow me, I've no idea where we are going' may not inspire anyone to follow. More often overlooked is that it's also necessary to sense where you currently are. Without that, you may under or overestimate the journey, or simply head in the wrong direction. But this is hard. Where we look with one eye at the destination, we cannot so easily see where we are now. When we look at where we are now, the destination can seem too far away.

When it comes to the journey itself, and we are forever journeying, it may be difficult to know what progress has been made, especially in an organisational culture in which people are trying to make it look as though they have done a good job, whether or not they really have done so. Without truth, all journeys are poorly mapped. Organisations try to have reporting systems that get to the truth, but some things, like cash, are easier to measure than others. The bottom line can obscure everything else.

In fact, leaders often have a fairly clear sense of where they want their organisation to go. They may say that the difficulty is in getting the organisation to go there. There is, however, often an underlying weakness: they don't know where they are, or rather they think they are in one place rather than another. We alluded to this problem when we described organisations in which leaders aren't told the truth about the way things are. This presents a problem: if you plan a route from Paris to Berlin but you are actually in London, you may be under-prepared for the journey. Knowing where you are in the present may be vital to getting to your future (Grint, 2005).

Many people believe it is harder to connect with future possibilities than to be in the present. Both may be difficult. As we have said, purpose provides one bridge into the future. Another is to seek to constantly improve everything: however good you have become, technology is likely to continue to provide new methods. Yet another is to make the future up. The great visionary leaders dream of what does not yet exist and share their dreams. Corporate leaders may dream too, but often need to keep their dreams confidential. Dreaming may be an underappreciated leadership capability, perhaps because – in a world where we are supposed to be doing 'hard work' – dreaming doesn't feel like work.

How can we resolve the paradox of being in the present and the future? One approach is to recognise them both and celebrate their differences: we exist in the present, that is clearly where we are, and we accept that the current reality is the current reality; we intend something rather different which does not yet exist, and we can accept that it doesn't yet exist, but we intend to move towards it. This applies to self, team and organisation. Although it is not yet truly real, we imagine that the future vision one day will be. And when one day it is, a new future starts to present itself, and so on, ad infinitum.

The paradoxes of team and time remain, but the discovery of purpose can provide a fresh perspective on both: when engaged in a noble purpose, identity becomes secondary. The same key takes us from the present into a congruent future. It's all a matter of purpose.

Questions for reflection and discussion

1. Starting with awareness, take 3–4 minutes to take note of what are you aware of right now in your surroundings and within yourself (thoughts, sounds, sensations, emotions, etc.). Have you noticed anything important or interesting that you were unaware of before? Write down your observations and, if studying in class, share them with others and discuss when you tend to be most present and alert and when are you most likely to be distracted.

2. How are you different from the person you were ten years ago? How would you like to be different from your current self, say, ten years from now? Write down your responses and identify an action plan for achieving your desired future.
3. Think about your experience of working in teams, can you identify times when you have felt part of the group and when you have felt separate from it? Do you notice any correlation between your response and your experiences of leading, co-leading and/or following?
4. What evidence do you have to suggest that leadership makes a difference in teams? What kind(s) of leadership is/are required, when, where, why and by whom? Write down as many ways as you can think of to get more active engagement within your team(s).
5. In what ways is the environment within which your team operates changing? What are the key priorities for you and your team to address in the next 3–4 years? What changes in team membership, capabilities and/or group dynamics are necessary in order to achieve your team's purpose? Write down your responses and identify an action plan.

Recommended reading

Bennis, Warren (1989) *On Becoming a Leader*, New York, NY: Addison Wesley.

Berne, E. (1964) *Games People Play: The Psychology of Human Relations*, Old Saybrook, CT: Tantor Books.

Goleman, D., Boyatzis, R. and McKee, A. (2002) *The New Leaders: Transforming the Art of Leadership into the Science of Results*, London: Little Brown.

Lencioni, P. (2002) *The Five Dysfunctions of a Team*, San Francisco, CA: Jossey-Bass.

Linacre, N. and Cann, J. (2011) *An Introduction to 3-Dimensional Leadership*, Chippenham: Extraordinary Leadership.

References

Aguilar, F.J. (1967) *Scanning the Business Environment*, New York, NY: Macmillan.

Alimo-Metcalfe, B. and Alban-Metcalfe, J. (2005) Leadership: Time for a New Direction, *Leadership* 1(1): 51–71.

Argyris, C. (1990) *Overcoming Organizational Defenses – Facilitating Organisational Learning*, New Jersey, NJ: Prentice Hall.

Berne, E. (1964) *Games People Play – the Psychology of Human Relations*, Old Saybrook, CT: Tantor Books.

Buckingham, M. and Coffman, C. (1999) *First, Break All the Rules: What the World's Greatest Managers Do Differently*, New York, NY: Simon & Schuster.

Collins, J. (2001) *Good to Great, Why Some Companies Make the Leap and Others Don't*, New York, NY: William Collins.

Dass, R. (1971) *Remember, Be Here Now*, San Cristobal, NM: Lama Foundation.

Duval, S. and Wicklund, R. (1972) *A Theory of Objective Self Awareness*, New York, NY: Academic Press.

Eden, T. (2013) *Prevolution, Rethinking Generation Y Leadership*, London: Blurb Books.

George, B. (2007) *True North, Discover Your Authentic Leadership*, San Francisco, CA: Wiley.

Goleman, D. (1996) *Emotional Intelligence, Why It Can Matter More Than IQ*, London: Bloomsbury Publishing.

Grint, K. (2005) *Leadership: Limits and Possibilities (Management, Work and Organisations)*, Basingstoke: Palgrave Macmillan.

Grint, K. (2008) *Wicked Problems and Clumsy Solutions: The Role of Leadership*, Stockport: BAMM (British Association of Medical Managers) Publications.

Haslam, A. (2004) *Psychology in Organizations: The Social Identity Approach*, London: Sage Publications.

Haslam, A. (2010) *The New Psychology of Leadership*, London: Psychology Press.

Johansen, B. (2012) *Leaders Make the Future: Ten New Leadership Skills for an Uncertain World*, San Francisco, CA: Berett-Koehler.

Kipling, R. (1910) If, in *Rewards and Fairies*, London: Macmillan.

Linacre, N. (1987) *Advertising for Account Handlers*, London: Random House.

Linacre N. and Cann, J. (2011) *An Introduction to 3-Dimensional Leadership*, Chippenham: Extraordinary Leadership.

McConaughey, M. (2014) Oscar acceptance speech.

Sinek, S. (2009) Start with Why. TED talk. Available at: www.youtube.com/watch?v=IPYeCltXpxw.

Voltaire (1759) *Candide, or All for the Best*, London: Wordsworth Press.

Vyasa, V. (100–500 BC) *Bhagavad Gita* [*Song of the Lord*], part of *Mahabharata*, Suny Press.

5

PARADOXICAL TRUTHS IN HEROIC LEADERSHIP

Implications for leadership development and effectiveness

Scott Allison and Jennifer Cecilione

In this chapter Scott Allison and Jennifer Cecilione explore the territory of heroic leadership, and the paradoxes therein. They take us through an understanding of the heroic leader's journey on to six leadership paradoxes concerning fact and fiction, visibility and invisibility, choosing leaders and being chosen, building and destroying, viewing and reviewing, and the light and dark sides of personality. Readers can explore how the hero's journey relates to their own. The authors have a depth of knowledge in psychology, Scott as a long-standing professor of psychology and author and speaker, and Jennifer as a psychology teaching fellow.

Introduction

Leadership is a complex social activity that implicates numerous, interconnected psychological and interpersonal processes (Goethals *et al.*, 2014). To understand leadership, scholars have rigorously studied the personality, vision, ethics, charisma and actions of leaders (Allison and Goethals, 2013). Leadership, of course, transcends individuality. A full understanding of leadership phenomena requires an appreciation of the broader group context that includes an examination of the reciprocal influences between leaders and followers (Messick, 2005), the myriad characteristics of followers (Armstrong, 2010), and the holistic environment in which leadership takes place (Padilla, 2012). The multi-level complexity of leadership poses such a great challenge to scholars and practitioners that hundreds of books have been written about leadership processes over the past two decades (Goethals *et al.*, 2014).

In this chapter, we discuss the basic elements of heroic leadership, showing how heroism and exemplary leadership are deeply intertwined. We then describe six paradoxical truths about heroic leadership that are often unrecognised and unappreciated. We believe that ignorance of these counterintuitive truths and paradoxes about heroic leadership can lead to misunderstandings about leaders, leadership and leadership development. Most of these paradoxes are a central part of the hero's journey as described by comparative mythologist Joseph Campbell (1949). We will discuss the genesis of these paradoxical truths, and we will suggest ways that an awareness of these principles can engender better leadership and more effective leadership development.[1]

Leadership and heroism

As research on leadership has proliferated over the past two decades, so has scholarly interest in positive psychology, a field that addresses optimal human functioning. Positive psychologists have shown a new (or renewed) interest in topics such as morality, cooperation, altruism, wisdom, meaning, purpose, resilience, hope, flow, human growth, courage, empathy, spirituality, health, public service, self-control, emotional intelligence and character strengths (Allison *et al.*, 2016). The past few years have witnessed a notable surge in research on one category of exceptional individuals who best exemplify these positive qualities: *heroes*. A hero is defined as a person who takes risks and makes self-sacrifices to better the lives of others (Allison and Goethals, 2011; Franco *et al.*, 2011). Not surprisingly, scholars have also defined a hero as a type of leader (Goethals and Allison, 2012). Heroes lead others either directly or indirectly by influencing people to follow their example in performing behaviours that save, protect or improve human lives. Thus, in this chapter, we use the terms *heroes* and *heroic leaders* interchangeably to refer to individuals who make positive and enduring contributions to organisations or to society.

A robust finding in psychology is that people are drawn to individuals who possess stereotypic characteristics of heroes and heroic leaders (Allison and Goethals, 2011, 2014; Goethals and Allison, 2014; Kinsella *et al.*, 2015). Defining these characteristics thus becomes vital to understanding heroes and heroic leaders. Freud (1922) conjectured that people assign leadership roles to men who represent the typical qualities of a group 'in a particularly clearly marked and pure form' and would often 'give an impression of greater force and of more freedom of libido' (p. 129). That is, leaders would be highly prototypical, unusually competent and extremely powerful. When we encounter people who resemble archetypical images of a hero, we endow them with heroic qualities and respond to them with strong positive emotions. Research shows that we react with reverence and awe to people who exude strong self-confidence and charisma (Goethals and Allison, 2014). Moreover, evolutionary theory suggests that individuals who emerged as leaders in early evolutionary time were 'big men' (Van Vugt *et al.*, 2008). Physically large males were perceived to be the most skilled, intelligent and effective in achieving the group's goals. Some of these primal conceptions of heroic leadership have endured, as even today tall people tend to be judged as more competent and as better leaders than are short people (Murray and Schmitz, 2011).

Psychological benefits of hero stories

Joseph Campbell (1949) was the first scholar to shed light on the psychological importance of hero stories and to offer insight about why we gravitate towards tales of heroism. According to Campbell, hero stories from every corner of the earth generally follow the same clear and predictable pattern. This universality prompted him to refer to the classic hero narrative as a *monomyth*, a single hero story to which all humans resonate. The monomythic hero story begins with an ordinary person, typically a male, who is summoned on a journey away from his safe, familiar world to a new and special world fraught with danger. At the outset of the journey, the hero is missing an important quality, usually courage, self-confidence, humility or a sense of an important life truth. The hero's journey is always a voyage towards self-realisation and transformation (Allison *et al.*, 2016; Smith and

Allison, 2014). Receiving assistance from enchanted and unlikely sources, the hero shows remarkable cunning, courage and resourcefulness to triumph. Once successful, the hero returns to his original familiar world to bestow a boon to the entire community.

Stories are psychologically powerful (Gardner, 1995; McAdams, 1997; Sternberg, 2011). Stories crystallise abstract concepts and endow them with contextual meaning (Boje, 1995). Sternberg (2011) and Gardner (1995) provide numerous examples of heroic leaders using stories to win the minds and hearts of their followers. Stories are more than tools for influencing others; they also promote self-change. McAdams (2014) has argued that personal self-narratives shape life trajectories and the maintenance of subjective well-being. For example, psychologists have found that war veterans suffering from PTSD are helped enormously by writing their personal stories of survival and recovery. Stories are rich, emotionally laden capsule summaries of wisdom for which the human mind was designed (Green and Brock, 2005; Haidt, 2012). According to Price (1978), 'a need to tell and hear stories is essential to the species Homo sapiens – second in necessity apparently after nourishment and before love and shelter' (p. 3).

The wisdom function of hero stories

Hero stories in particular fulfil two principal human functions: a *wisdom* function and an *energising* function (Allison and Goethals, 2014, 2015). The wisdom function refers to the knowledge and insights that hero stories impart to us. Stories of heroic action bestow wisdom by supplying mental models, or scripts, for how to nobly lead one's life. Heroic narratives also teach us how we should behave in crisis situations (Allison and Goethals, 2011; Goethals and Allison, 2012). Yet, hero narratives are more than simple scripts prescribing prosocial action. Joseph Campbell believed that the classic hero monomyth reveals life's deepest psychological truths (Mishlove, 1998). Hero stories reveal deep truths in several ways. First, tales of heroism send readers into *deep time*, meaning that the truths contained in hero stories enjoy a timelessness that connects us with the past, the present and the future. Rohr (2011) notes that deep time is evident when stories contain phrases such as 'Once upon a time', 'A long time ago in a galaxy far, far away' and 'they lived happily ever after'. A second way that hero stories emphasise deep truth is by emphasising *deep roles* in our social fabric. Moxnes (1999) has argued that the deepest roles portrayed widely in hero stories are archetypal family roles such as mother, child, maiden and wise old man or grandparent.

Many of the lessons to be gleaned from hero stories are not always so apparent. Another wisdom function of hero stories resides in their ability to shed light on meaningful life paradoxes. People have trouble unpacking the value of paradoxical truths unless the contradictions contained within the paradoxes are illustrated inside a compelling story. Campbell (1949) believed that stories are saturated with paradox, as evidenced in his famous utterance, 'where you stumble, there lies your treasure' (p. 75). Only when heroes summon the courage to face their challenges do they undergo the personal transformation needed to complete their hero journey. According to Campbell, our hero journeys involve letting go of our false selves or former selves and allowing our true heroic selves to emerge. Counterintuitively, the journey requires a departure from the comforts of home into a strange, uncomfortable and dangerous world (Campbell, 1988). Embarking on this pilgrimage is the surest path to growth and transformation, and hero stories teach us, whether we are heroes or not, that we must all leave our safe, familiar worlds to find our true selves (Levinson, 1978).

In addition to teaching us a way to discover our true selves, hero stories improve our emotional intelligence. Also known as EQ, emotional intelligence refers to people's ability to identify, understand, use and manage emotions (Mayer *et al.*, 2001). Psychoanalyst Bruno Bettelheim believed that children's fairytales are useful in helping people, especially children, understand emotional experience (Bettelheim, 1976). The heroes of these fairytales are usually subjected to dark, foreboding experiences, such as encounters with witches, evil spells, abandonment, neglect, abuse and death. The audience vicariously experiences these dark stimuli, allowing them to develop strategies for resolving their own fears and distresses. Bettelheim (1976) believed that even the most distressing fairytales, such as those by the Brothers Grimm, add clarity and salience to confusing emotions and give people a greater sense of life's meaning and purpose.

A final wisdom benefit of hero stories is in their focus on the essential role of sacrifice in the hero's journey and in human growth and development. Franco *et al.* (2011) have claimed that self-sacrifice may be the principal defining feature of heroism, and they argue that sacrifice distinguishes heroism from altruism. Campbell (1949, 1988) emphasised the importance of sacrifice in the hero's journey and observed that self-sacrifice is an integral element of hero myths around the globe. Ancient Greek and Roman religious practices revolved around sacrificial ceremonies during which animals were killed and eaten to show respect for, and earn peace with, the gods. In the *Odyssey*, Odysseus must plant his oar into the ground and sacrifice a ram, a bull and a boar to Neptune. Rohr (2011) has argued that this sacrifice reflects Homer's belief that all great heroes cannot complete their heroic task unless they give up tangible symbols of youthful priorities. A battering ram, a breeding bull and a wild boar are vivid symbols of immature male energy that must be outgrown and sacrificed for Odysseus to develop into a true elder and heroic leader of Ithaca.

The energising function of hero stories

Hero stories do more than just teach us important lessons; they also energise and inspire us. Recent work suggests that heroes and heroic action evoke a unique emotional response that Jonathan Haidt and his colleagues have called *elevation* (Algoe and Haidt, 2009; Haidt, 2003). When people experience elevation, they feel a mix of awe, reverence and admiration for a morally beautiful act (Gray and Wegner, 2011). The emotion is described as similar to calmness, warmth and love. Haidt (2003) argues that elevation is 'elicited by acts of virtue or moral beauty; it causes warm, open feelings in the chest' (p. 276). Most importantly, the feeling of elevation has a concomitant behavioural component: a desire to become a better person. Elevation 'motivates people to behave more virtuously themselves' (Haidt, 2003, p. 276). A form of moral self-efficacy, elevation transforms people into believing they are capable of significant prosocial action (Britton, 2008).

Besides promoting elevation, hero stories serve an important healing function. Storytelling is known to be a community-building activity (Price, 1978). For early humans, the act of gathering around communal fires to hear stories established social connections with others. This sense of family, group or community still remains central to human emotional well-being (Leary and Baumeister, 2000). The content of hero stories also promotes a strong sense of social identity. Effective heroes perform actions that exemplify and affirm the community's most cherished values. The validation of a shared worldview, displayed vividly through storytelling, alleviates doubts and distress as well as builds self-esteem (Solomon *et al.*, 2014).

Hero stories also inspire us to give back and make positive changes to the world. Campbell's (1949) stages of the hero's journey culminate with the gift, boon or elixir that the hero bestows upon the community from which he originated. Both Campbell and Erikson (1975) believed that personal transformation is the key to reaching the *generativity* stage of human development, during which people generously give back to the society that has given them so much. In effective hero stories, the key to achieving transformation is the discovery of an important missing inner quality that has heretofore hindered personal growth. Good heroes use the power of transformation not only to change themselves for the better, but also to transform the world in which they live. Campbell (1988) describes the power of mythic transformation in this way:

> If you realize what the real problem is—losing yourself, giving yourself to some higher end, or to another—you realize that this itself is the ultimate trial. When we quit thinking primarily about ourselves and our own self-preservation, we undergo a truly heroic transformation of consciousness. And what all the myths have to deal with is transformations of consciousness of one kind or another.
>
> *(p. 112)*

Moreover, hero stories energise and change us by featuring a hero who is an underdog or 'everyman' summoned on a journey fraught with extraordinary challenges. Our research on underdogs shows that we identify with them, root for them, and judge them to be highly inspiring when they triumph (Allison and Burnette, 2009; Allison and Goethals, 2008; Davis *et al.*, 2011; Kim *et al.*, 2008; Vandello *et al.*, 2007). Research conducted by Kinsella *et al.* (2015) suggests that the inspiring quality of heroes is what distinguishes heroes from altruists, helpers and leaders. Consistent with this idea,

Allison and Goethals (2011) used factor and cluster-analytic statistical procedures to uncover eight general categories of traits that describe heroes that they coined as *The Great Eight*. These trait categories consist of *smart*, *strong*, *charismatic*, *reliable*, *resilient*, *selfless*, *caring* and *inspiring*. When asked which of the great eight are the most important descriptors of heroes, a different group of participants reported that the trait of *inspiring* is the most important of the eight (Allison and Goethals, 2011).

Paradoxes of heroism

G.K. Chesterton described paradox as 'a truth that stands on her head to gain attention' (Douglas, 2001). We agree with Joseph Campbell (1949) that hero stories are rife with paradoxical truths, and we further contend that an understanding of these paradoxical truths is essential for the implementation of effective leadership development practices. Below we describe six such paradoxes and how they can be used to improve the way we view leaders, follow leaders, and become leaders ourselves.

Paradox 1: the truest heroes are fictional heroes

Our research on heroes has revealed an important insight about the distinction between heroes of fiction and heroes of non-fiction. We conducted a study in which we asked people to rate the goodness (or badness) of heroes and villains. Some of the heroes and villains that people rated were fictional, whereas others were real-life heroes and villains. Our results showed that fictional heroes and villains were rated as more extremely good or bad than their real-world counterparts (Allison and Goethals, 2011). In short, fictional heroes are more archetypal or 'truer' heroes. We suspect that the creators of fiction draw from classic prototypes of good and evil when constructing their characters. While elements of these exemplars can surely be found in real-world heroes and villains, fictional stereotypes are more cleanly drawn with their essential features accentuated. This exaggerated prototypical nature of fictional heroes may explain why people are drawn so strongly to comic book superheroes, whose amplified abilities and virtues hold such alluring appeal.

Being cognisant of the hero archetype has significant implications for leadership. Highly effective leaders know that framing their lives and their careers in the context of a good hero story will bring them greater success. Leaders develop personal narratives and use hero characteristics to convey a powerful message that will move followers emotionally and behaviourally (Gardner, 1995; Sternberg, 2011). To maximise the effectiveness of the message, the hero of the story should acquire and retain as many traits that are prototypical of heroism as possible. Ideally, the leader has (1) undertaken some type of risky journey; (2) made significant self-sacrifices along the way; (3) discovered something important about himself or herself and the world; (4) undergone a momentous personal transformation; (5) developed a deep, altruistic desire to share the gift of this discovery with the world; and (6) as a result of the journey, acquired heroic traits such as strength, courage, wisdom, resilience, loyalty and generosity.

Paradox 2: the most abundant heroes are also the most invisible

An important type of hero is called the *transparent hero*, who does his or her heroic work behind the scenes, outside the public spotlight (Goethals and Allison, 2012). Transparent heroes include teachers, coaches, mentors, healthcare workers, law enforcement personnel, firefighters and military personnel. Although these heroes are found in abundance, they largely go unnoticed and are our most unsung heroic leaders.

These hidden heroes make miracles happen everyday but also go unrecognised.

It may appear unbelievable that transparent heroes so frequently go unnoticed and underappreciated despite their charitable behaviour. A cognitive bias called the *negativity bias* (Baumeister *et al.*, 2001) may help explain this unjust and unfathomable phenomenon. This bias refers to the human tendency to show greater sensitivity to negative information about people than about positive information. For instance, if one is given both good and bad information about someone, one is more likely to pay attention to the bad information and to remember it more so than the good information. Additionally, the bad information will carry more weight in impressions of that person. Psychologists have also found that negative experiences in our lives have more emotional impact on us than positive ones (Baumeister *et al.*, 2001). If people have a good and a bad experience close together in time, they are more likely to feel worse than if they have two neutral experiences.

To the extent that we show the negativity bias in our perceptions of the world, the salience of good behaviour will always be drowned out by bad behaviour even if there is a much greater preponderance of good behaviour. For this reason, transparent heroes will go about doing their heroic work unnoticed and unsung. Fortunately, transparent heroes are not motivated by fame and fortune. Instead, they are intrinsically motivated to do their jobs of healing, nurturing and protecting simply because they know it is the right thing to do. If they were motivated by money or fanfare, they would most certainly pursue an alternative form of heroism. Leaders should always remember that the most vital lesson of the transparent hero is that of humility. Although it is crucial for leaders to accentuate their positive qualities, leaders must do so in the role of the humble servant for whom service to others is not the means to an end but is the end itself.

Paradox 3: we do not choose our heroes; they choose us

As we have noted earlier, people are drawn to individuals who possess stereotypic characteristics of heroes and heroic leaders. More than half a century ago, Carl Jung (1954) proposed the idea that all humans have collectively inherited unconscious images, ideas, or thoughts, which he called *archetypes*. These archetypes reflect common experiences that all humans (and their ancestors) have shared over millions of years of evolution. The main purpose of these archetypes is to prepare us for common experiences. Two such archetypes, according to Jung, are *heroes* and *demons*. Current research appears to support Jung – scientists have found that newborn babies are equipped with a readiness for language, for numbers, and for their parents' faces. Recent findings also show that young infants exhibit a preference for moral behaviour over immoral behaviour (Hamlin, 2013). Humans appear to be innately prepared for certain people and tasks, and we believe this may include encounters with heroes.

Archetypes prepare us for the process of identifying and choosing heroes and leaders. These archetypes produce the following paradox: because our minds are innately equipped with images of the looks, traits and behaviours of heroes, our leaders and heroes may choose us as much as we choose them. One implication of this paradox is that leaders can develop a keen understanding of followers' archetypal sensitivities, which will allow them to better attract followers and meet their needs. Jung's research on archetypes suggests that we can learn to trust our instincts about good leadership and heroism. At the same time, we must be careful not to be misled by our instincts, as appearances can be deceiving. An incompetent leader who is tall and charismatic can fool us into believing he is an effective leader. We must also be careful in never using what we know about leadership archetypes to exploit others. Authentic leadership involves using knowledge of archetypes to improve one's ability to motivate and connect with followers.

Paradox 4: we love to build up our heroes, and we also love to destroy them

People are thirsty for heroes because heroes offer hope. Our research shows that dramatic tales of heroes rising into prominence, especially when these heroes are underdogs who prevail against the odds, captivate audiences. We cherish heroes and seemingly go out of our way to construct them. But the reverse is also true. We appear to crave the undoing of heroes as well. Our studies show that our greatest heroes cannot get away with anything less than near-perfect moral behaviour. For this reason, many heroes are bound to fall from grace. We seem to believe in, and relish, a perverse law of heroic gravity: what goes up must come down. The rising of the hero is a central part of the hero narrative that imparts wisdom about how to succeed and prevail amidst adversity. Likewise, the falling of the hero imparts wisdom by offering us a cautionary tale about the consequences of succumbing to human vices.

The implication for leadership development is the importance of remembering that leaders are held to a higher standard of ethical conduct than are non-leaders. Moral transgressions, even minor ones, can destroy a revered leader's career and legacy. Followers have a low tolerance for, and a heightened sensitivity to, heroic leaders who behave immorally in the slightest degree. Allison and Goethals (2015) propose a psychological reason for this sensitivity to leader misbehaviour. They theorise that followers believe that an implicit contract exists between themselves and heroic leaders. This implied contract stipulates that followers will give heroes their adoration as long as the heroes behave virtuously. When heroes engage in a moral transgression, followers interpret the transgression as a violation of the contract, thereby giving followers permission to terminate their adoration. Therefore, heroes and leaders must be mindful of this tacit contract or else they risk tarnishing their reputation and credibility.

Paradox 5: we love heroes the most when they are gone

The results of many studies underscore the role of death in shaping our affections towards heroes. As much as we love our heroes when they are alive and well, we love them even more when they are dead. We call this phenomenon *the death positivity bias* (Eylon and Allison, 2005). Elevated posthumous evaluations may contribute significantly to people's beliefs about the heroism in a leader. Research has shown that getting assassinated truly helps a leader gain stature as a stirring legend (Simonton, 1994). The most cherished of our heroes often must die to achieve their greatness. Moreover, the cause of death influences how we evaluate deceased leaders. Our research has shown that leaders who die from a prolonged illness are evaluated the most favourably, presumably because we sympathise with their suffering. The death positivity bias is almost as strong for leaders who are assassinated or who die in accidents. The bias is smallest for leaders who commit suicide.

Obviously, we do not encourage leaders to die to maximise their impact, although that would appear to be the comically morbid conclusion to reach from our research. Instead, we encourage organisations to capitalise on great leadership from the past to motivate and inspire followers. In America, Ford Motor Company uses stories of legendary founder Henry Ford to tell a stirring and heroic message of sacrifice and innovation for the benefit of followers. Apple Computers does the same with former CEO Steve Jobs. Current leaders need not die to inspire their followers but they can resurrect the genius of past leadership to stimulate followers and create a vision for organisations.

Paradox 6: sometimes the darkest side of a leader's personality produces the brightest leadership

As we have noted earlier, positive psychologists have directed their attention to human traits that promote the most admirable heroic behaviour. These traits include courage, empathy, wisdom, kindness and other inspiring qualities (Allison *et al.*, 2016). Paradoxically, some psychologists have discovered that several personality traits associated with psychopathy have also been linked to success in business, politics and even professional sports. Vitelli (2012) has observed, for example, that psychopaths and heroes share the trait of *fearlessness*. Vitelli (2012) also notes that President Lyndon Baines Johnson and British Prime Minister Winston Churchill demonstrated traits that could be considered 'psychopathological'. For instance, early in their careers Johnson and Churchill were daring, adventurous and unconventional young men who began playing by their own rules. Later, they mellowed into respected politicians after learning to effectively harness these traits.

The dark side of human nature may sometimes produce the brightest leadership. Moreover, there may be a paradox within this paradox. People tend to admire rule-breakers if they get away with their transgressions, and this fact could be part of the appeal of both Johnson and Churchill. Maradona is a much-admired football player in Argentina precisely because he broke the rules and got away with it, in much the same way that Robin Hood was a much-admired outlaw in medieval England. Lilienfeld *et al.* (2012) found that fearless dominance, which is also considered to be a psychopathic characteristic, is linked to the success of many American presidents, especially during times of crisis management. These investigators argue that fearless dominance is a telling attribute of high-functioning psychopaths who are able to thrive as leaders in business settings. Paradoxically, personality traits associated with human pathology can sometimes be useful – if harnessed towards a noble end – to engender the brightest leadership. Leaders should understand and anticipate that expressing a trait such as fearless dominance may be necessary during times of emergency and turmoil.

Summary and conclusions

In this chapter, we have borrowed wisdom gleaned from the classic hero narrative to generate lessons for leadership development and leadership effectiveness. Many of these lessons are nonobvious because they stem from paradoxical truths about the hero's journey. These lessons include the idea that (1) fictional heroes can teach us as much or more about heroic leadership than can real-world heroes; (2) the most invisible heroes among us underscore the timeless principle that humble unsung service to others is a central goal of leadership; (3) a keen understanding of the hero archetype can help leaders cultivate connections with others and foster their ability to motivate others to action; (4) leaders must always honour their part of the implicit contract that exists between them and their followers by leading ethically and responsibly at all times; (5) leaders should consider harnessing the genius of past leadership to stimulate followers and to promote a vision for organisations; and (6) leaders can utilise some personality traits associated with human pathology, such as fearless dominance, for good use during times of crisis.

Campbell (1949) believed that the monomyth of the hero contains rich insights about the deepest psychological needs and desires of humanity. Leaders who acknowledge their followers' needs and desires can lead with greater effectiveness. We have shown how human beings resonate well to notions of *deep time* and *deep roles*, which remind us of ageless truths about living and working together in the most optimal, harmonious and productive ways. We have also demonstrated the crucial importance of *sacrifice* in the hero's journey, and we encourage leaders to make rousing accounts of past sacrifices an integral part of their organisation's story.

The mythic hero's journey has yet to be fully mined for its insights about leadership and followership. Central to the classic hero narrative is the idea that heroes are missing a vital inner quality when they first embark on their journeys. This quality is essential for their success; thus, heroes must experience suffering because they are ill-equipped to handle the challenges they face. Campbell (1949) emphasises the role of a mentor figure who appears before the hero to help him or her discover, or recover, the missing quality. This mentorship, of course, represents the leadership component of the hero's journey. Paradoxically, then, hero stories teach us that setback and suffering are necessary for progress and growth. The leader's mission in any organisation is to serve as a mentor for followers, helping them discover and develop qualities that they are missing. We encourage leaders to humbly recognise that they are not the heroes; rather, they are the mentors who are assisting in the transformation of followers, who are themselves in the early stages of their own hero journeys.

The ultimate paradox of leadership may reside in the idea that one must 'give it away to keep it'. This spiritual principle is a core principle of Alcoholics Anonymous's twelfth step, which encourages members to stay in sobriety by passing along the knowledge of their recovery programme to others. One's own gifts are best retained by offering them to others. Consequently, one of the greatest strategies for becoming a heroic leader is to assist in the development of heroic leadership in others. James MacGregor Burns (1978, 2003) called this process *transformational leadership*. Having once been mentored into greatness, our most heroic leaders understand that their current role in the hero journey is to help transform others and the greater society to which they belong.

Questions for reflection and discussion

1. How can you use the classic hero's journey to maximise your effectiveness as a leader? First, consider which aspects of your personal and professional life parallel the classic hero's journey. What unique challenges have you faced and conquered? What positive traits were you compelled to cultivate as a result of these challenges? What heroic mentors have provided invaluable assistance to you on your journey? What valuable life lessons (and organisational lessons) have you learned from these mentors? In what ways have you used the wisdom you have gleaned from past mentors to improve your leadership and/or your organisation?
2. How can you use Paradox 1 – the truest heroes are fictional heroes – to enhance the effectiveness of your leadership? Specifically, what risks have you taken to foster better leadership? What sacrifices have you made? What important self-discoveries have you come to that have served you well on your personal and professional journey? In what ways have you been transformed, either personally or professionally? Have you shared your new-found gifts with others or used those gifts to help transform others?

3. How can you use Paradox 2 – the most abundant heroes are the most invisible – to improve your leadership? The most important lesson of the transparent hero is that of humility. Although it is important for leaders to accentuate their positive qualities, leaders must do so in the role of the humble servant for whom service to others is not the means to an end but is the end itself. With all of your successes, how have you remained humble? In what ways are you careful to cultivate a non-arrogant image of yourself and of your organisation? Do you make sure that you are of service to others, both within and outside of your organisation?
4. How can you use Paradox 3 – we do not choose our leaders, they choose us – to augment your leadership effectiveness? What practices do you employ to ensure that your leadership is authentic and not contrived? Are you careful not to show biases in the hiring and training of managers? Are your leadership practices based on substantive criteria and not simply on superficial appearance?
5. In what ways can you use Paradox 4 – we love to build up our heroes and we also love to destroy them – to improve your leadership? Do you take steps to ensure that you follow the highest standards of ethical conduct? Do you ensure that your leadership team knows that any transgressions, even minor ones, can destroy a career and legacy? Develop an action plan for making every person who occupies a leadership position in your organisation aware of the implicit contract that exists between themselves and their followers. Remember that the implied contract stipulates that followers will give heroes their loyalty as long as the heroes behave virtuously.
6. How can you use Paradox 5 – we love heroes the most when they are gone – to maximise the effectiveness of your organisation? How can you capitalise on great leadership from the past in your organisation to motivate and inspire current followers? What are the inspiring qualities of these past leaders and how can you tap into those qualities to precipitate positive change in your organisation today? Develop a plan for resurrecting the genius of past leadership in your organisation to stimulate followers thereby creating a vision for greatness in your organisation.
7. What lessons for effectiveness leadership can be gleaned from Paradox 6 – sometimes the darkest side of a leader's personality

produces the brightest leadership? What personality traits associated with human pathology might at times be useful – if harnessed towards a noble end – to engender the brightest leadership in your organisation? Have any past or present leaders in your organisations taken a controversial stand on an issue and were later shown to be pioneers who were ahead of their time? Could you use this genius to bolster your current organisation's direction? Is current leadership in your organisation lacking the trait of *fearlessness*? Could leaders in your unit benefit from more judicious risk-taking? Is the leadership in your organisation so opposed to risk that bold, new, creative ideas are discouraged? Develop an action plan for encouraging the generation of daring new ideas from both leaders and followers in your organisation with the idea that heroic leadership involves revolutionary thinking and intelligent risk-taking.

Note

1 The research summarised in this chapter was supported by a John Templeton Foundation Grant (#35279) awarded to Scott T. Allison.

Recommended reading

Allison, S.T. and Goethals, G.R. (2011). *Heroes: What they do and why we need them*. New York, NY: Oxford University Press.

Allison, S.T. and Goethals, G.R. (2013). *Heroic leadership: an influence taxonomy of 100 exceptional individuals*. New York, NY: Routledge.

Allison, S.T., Goethals, G.R. and Kramer, R.M. (eds) (2016). *Handbook of heroism and heroic leadership*. New York, NY: Routledge.

Franco, Z.E., Blau, K. and Zimbardo, P.G. (2011). Heroism: a conceptual analysis and differentiation between heroic action and altruism. *Review of General Psychology*. doi: 10.1037/a0022672.

Goethals, G.R., Allison, S.T., Kramer, R.M. and Messick, D.M. (eds) (2014). *Conceptions of leadership: enduring ideas and emerging insights*. New York, NY: Palgrave Macmillan.

References

Algoe, S.B. and Haidt, J. (2009). Witnessing excellence in action: the 'other-praising' emotions of elevation, gratitude, and admiration. *Journal of Positive Psychology*, 4, 105–127.

Allison, S.T. and Burnette, J. (2009). Fairness and preference for underdogs and top dogs. In R. Kramer, A. Tenbrunsel and M. Bazerman (eds), *Social decision making: social dilemmas, social values, and ethical judgments* (pp. 112–138). New York, NY: Psychology Press.

Allison, S.T. and Goethals, G.R. (2008). Deifying the dead and downtrodden: sympathetic figures as inspirational leaders. In C.L. Hoyt, G.R. Goethals and D.R. Forsyth (eds), *Leadership at the crossroads: psychology and leadership* (pp. 160–177). Westport, CT: Praeger.

Allison, S.T. and Goethals, G.R. (2011). *Heroes: what they do and why we need them*. New York, NY: Oxford University Press.

Allison, S.T. and Goethals, G.R. (2013). *Heroic leadership: an influence taxonomy of 100 exceptional individuals*. New York, NY: Routledge.

Allison, S.T. and Goethals, G.R. (2014). 'Now he belongs to the ages': the heroic leadership dynamic and deep narratives of greatness. In G. Goethals, S. Allison, R. Kramer and D. Messick (eds), *Conceptions of leadership: enduring ideas and emerging insights* (pp. 167–184). New York, NY: Palgrave Macmillan.

Allison, S.T. and Goethals, G.R. (2015). Hero worship: the elevation of the human spirit. *The Journal for the Theory of Social Behaviour*. doi: 10.1111/jtsb.12094.

Allison, S.T., Goethals, G.R. and Kramer, R.M. (eds) (2016). *Handbook of heroism and heroic leadership*. New York, NY: Routledge.

Allison, S.T., Kocher, C.T. and Goethals, G.R. (eds) (2016). *The better angels of our nature: frontiers in spiritual leadership*. New York, NY: Palgrave Macmillan.

Armstrong, T. (2010). *Followership*. Shippensburg, PA: Destiny Images Publishers.

Baumeister, R.F., Bratslavsky, E., Finkenauer, C. and Vohs, K. (2001). Bad is stronger than good. *Review of General Psychology*, 5, 323–370.

Bettelheim, B. (1976). *The uses of enchantment: the meaning and importance of fairy tales*. New York, NY: Knopf.

Boje, D.M. (1995). Stories of the storytelling organization: a postmodern analysis of Disney as Tamara-land. *Academy of Management Journal*, 38, 997–1035.

Britton, K. (2008). Awe and elevation. *Positive Psychology News Daily*. Retrieved on 1 March 2013 from http://positivepsychologynews.com/news/kathryn-britton/20080507738.

Burns, J.M. (1978). *Leadership*. New York, NY: Harper & Row.

Burns, J.M. (2003). *Transforming leadership*. New York, NY: Atlantic Monthly Press.

Campbell, J. (1949). *The hero with a thousand faces*. New York, NY: New World Library.

Campbell, J. (1988). *The power of myth, with Bill Moyers*. New York, NY: Doubleday.

Davis, J.L., Burnette, J.L., Allison, S.T. and Stone, H. (2011). Against the odds: academic underdogs benefit from incremental theories. *Social Psychology of Education*, 14, 331–346.

Douglas, J.D. (2001). *G.K. Chesterton, the eccentric prince of paradox*. Retrieved on 8 March 2015 from http://bit.ly/1Tu3TLH.

Erikson, E.H. (1975). *Life history and the historical moment*. New York, NY: Norton.

Eylon, D. and Allison, S.T. (2005). The frozen in time effect in evaluations of the dead. *Personality and Social Psychology Bulletin*, 31, 1708–1717.

Franco, Z.E., Blau, K. and Zimbardo, P.G. (2011). Heroism: a conceptual analysis and differentiation between heroic action and altruism. *Review of General Psychology*, 5, 99–113.

Freud, S. (1922). Group psychology and the analysis of the ego. In J. Strachey (ed.), *The standard edition of the complete works of Sigmund Freud, V. 28, beyond the pleasure principle, group psychology, and other works* (pp. 45–112). London: Hogarth Press.

Gardner, H.E. (1995). *Leading minds: an anatomy of leadership*. New York, NY: Basic Books.

Goethals, G.R. and Allison, S.T. (2012). Making heroes: the construction of courage, competence and virtue. *Advances in Experimental Social Psychology*, 46, 183–235.

Goethals, G.R. and Allison, S.T. (2014). Kings and charisma, Lincoln and leadership: an evolutionary perspective. In G.R. Goethals, S.T. Allison, R. Kramer and D. Messick (eds), *Conceptions of leadership: enduring ideas and emerging insights* (pp. 111–126). New York, NY: Palgrave Macmillan.

Goethals, G.R., Allison, S.T., Kramer, R.M. and Messick, D.M. (eds) (2014). *Conceptions of leadership: enduring ideas and emerging insights*. New York, NY: Palgrave Macmillan.

Gray, K. and Wegner, D.M. (2011). Dimensions of moral emotions. *Emotion Review*, 3, 258–260.

Green, M.C. and Brock, T.C. (2005). Persuasiveness of narratives. In M.C. Green and T.C. Brock (eds), *Persuasion: psychological insights and perspectives* (pp. 117–142). Thousand Oaks, CA: Sage.

Haidt, J. (2003). Elevation and the positive psychology of morality. In C.L.M. Keyes and J. Haidt (eds), *Flourishing: positive psychology and the life well-lived* (pp. 275–289). Washington, DC: American Psychological Association.

Haidt, J. (2012). *The righteous mind: why good people are divided by politics and religion*. New York, NY: Pantheon.

Hamlin, J.K. (2013). Moral judgment and action in preverbal infants and toddlers: evidence for an innate moral core. *Current Directions in Psychological Science*, 22, 186–193.

Jung, C.G. (1954). *The archetypes and the collective unconscious* (1981 2nd edn, *Collected works*, Vol. 9, Part 1). Princeton, NJ: Bollingen.

Kim, J., Allison, S.T., Eylon, D., Goethals, G., Markus, M., McGuire, H. and Hindle, S. (2008). Rooting for (and then abandoning) the underdog. *Journal of Applied Social Psychology*, 38, 2550–2573.

Kinsella, E.L., Ritchie, T.D. and Igou, E.R. (2015). Zeroing in on heroes: a prototype analysis of hero features. *Journal of Personality and Social Psychology*, 108, 114–127.

Leary, M.R. and Baumeister, R.F. (2000). The nature and function of self-esteem: sociometer theory. In M. Zanna (ed.), *Advances in experimental social psychology*, Vol. 32 (pp. 1–62). San Diego, CA: Academic Press.

Levinson, D.J. (1978). *Seasons of a man's life*. New York, NY: Random House.

Lilienfeld, S.O., Waldman, I., Landfield, K., Watts, A., Rubenzer, S. and Faschingbauer, T. (2012). Fearless dominance and the U.S. presidency:

implications of psychopathic personality traits for successful and unsuccessful political leadership. *Journal of Personality and Social Psychology*, 103, 489–505.

McAdams, D.P. (1997). *The stories we live by: personal myths and the making of the self*. New York, NY: Guilford Press.

McAdams, D.P. (2014). Leaders and their life stories: Obama, Bush, and narratives of redemption. In G.R. Goethals, S.T. Allison, R. Kramer and D. Messick (eds), *Conceptions of leadership: enduring ideas and emerging insights* (pp. 147–166). New York, NY: Palgrave Macmillan.

Mayer, J.D., Salovey, P., Caruso, D.L. and Sitarenios, G. (2001). Emotional intelligence as a standard intelligence. *Emotion*, 1, 232–242.

Messick, D.M. (2005). On the psychological exchange between leaders and followers. In D.M. Messick and R.M. Kramer (eds), *The psychology of leadership: new perspectives and research* (pp. 81–96). Mahwah: Lawrence Erlbaum.

Mishlove, J. (1998). *Thinking allowed: conversations on the leading edge of knowledge and discovery*. Retrieved on 5 March 2014 from www.williamjames.com/transcripts/campbell.htm.

Moxnes, P. (1999). Deep roles: twelve primordial roles of mind and organization. *Human Relations*, 52, 1427–1444.

Murray, G.R. and Schmitz, J.D. (2011). Caveman politics: evolutionary leadership preferences and physical stature. *Social Science Quarterly*, 92, 1215–1235.

Padilla, A. (2012). *Leadership: leaders, followers, environments*. New York, NY: Wiley.

Price, R. (1978). *A palpable God*. New York, NY: Atheneum.

Rohr, R. (2011). *Falling upward*. New York, NY: Jossey-Bass.

Simonton, D.K. (1994). *Greatness: who makes history and why*. New York, NY: Guilford Press.

Smith, G. and Allison, S.T. (2014). *Reel heroes: volume 1: two hero experts critique the movies*. Richmond: Agile Writer Press.

Solomon, S., Greenberg, J., Schimel, J., Arndt, J. and Pyszczynski, T. (2014). *Human awareness of mortality and the evolution of culture*. Unpublished manuscript.

Sternberg, R.J. (2011). Leadership and education: leadership stories. In M. Harvey and R. Riggio (eds), *Leadership studies: the dialogue of disciplines* (pp. 88–101). New York, NY: Edward Elgar.

Van Vugt, M., Johnson, D.D.P., Kaiser, R.B. and O'Gorman, R. (2008). Evolution and the social psychology of leadership: the mismatch hypothesis. In C.L. Hoyt, G.R. Goethals and D.R. Forsyth (eds), *Leadership at the crossroads, volume 1, leadership and psychology* (pp. 102–119). Westport, CT: Praeger.

Vandello, J.A., Goldschmied, N.P. and Richards, D.A.R. (2007). The appeal of the underdog. *Personality and Social Psychology Bulletin*, 33, 1603–1616.

Vitelli, R. (2012). *Can psychopathic personality traits predict successful presidents?* Retrieved on 8 March 2015 from http://bit.ly/1Wl5HWk.

6

THE LEADER'S CONUNDRUM

A paradox of distortion

John Lawler and Jeff Gold

John Lawler and Jeff Gold argue that we confuse leaders with leadership. The consequent focus on the development of individual leaders creates a paradox of distortion. They offer what they call the leader's conundrum, which describes the process whereby senior leaders seek to control events and in so doing suffer a loss of control. Combining practice and theory, John Lawler brings his experience of helping business leaders plan and implement team alignment during points of transition, while Jeff Gold is Professor of Organisational Learning at Leeds Beckett University and has written extensively in this field.

Introduction

It has been a notable feature of the last 30 years how 'leader' rather than 'manager' has become a preferred label, or perhaps a re-label to provide more attraction and impression in fast moving times (Alvesson and Spicer, 2012). Nevertheless, before, during and after the 2007/8 Global Financial Crisis (GFC), a great deal was expected of those senior figures in organisations who were the leaders. Indeed, for much of the last 30 years, the image of an effective leader has been strongly associated with people who could create pride, respect and trust amongst followers, who in turn would be motivated to perform beyond expectations. Such leaders matched the categorisation of 'transformational' or 'charismatic-transformational' (Bass, 1985), and this image was credited with a 'rejuvenation of the leadership field' (Hunt, 1999, p. 129). Once this idea took hold, a great deal of energy was expended to show the evidence for the effectiveness of transformational leaders, providing the means to help recognise who could become transformational leaders and providing the learning and development that meant they became transformational leaders.

There are of course other images of leaders. What is most striking about these is that they tend to focus on particular individuals who can be assessed, selected and developed for senior roles where they will perform as leaders. This suggests that the leaders do the leadership. However, for us, this produces a rather important paradox. In this chapter, we will argue that the concentration on particular individuals as leaders, along with a devotion of resources to their development is, at the same time, a distortion of leadership practice. We will argue that when those appointed as leaders seek to control the direction of events, such as during projects of change, they are also likely to suffer a loss of control, which in turn produces an ongoing cycle that seeks to find ways for leaders to (re)assert control, as part of the myth that individual leaders can be in control. We present this as the leader's conundrum. We will begin with a brief overview of the tradition of leadership, before considering a counter-tradition. This provides the source of the leader's conundrum which lays the trap for the paradox of distortion. We will make use of the metaphor of a river and riverbank, drawn from the philosophy of Wittgenstein, in the examination of the working of leadership during projects of change.

Leaders . . .

Throughout the twentieth century and into the twenty-first, leadership has been the Holy Grail for management researchers and commentators. Leadership has been the single biggest issue for discussion within management journals and a 'hot topic' or 'panacea' of our times (Bolden *et al.*, 2011). However, for much of this time, and we suspect for most readers of this chapter, a basic identity has applied:

Leaders = Leadership

Seeing leaders *as* leadership can create a simplified perspective, attributing both success (in terms of a link to organisation performance) and failure (Kelley, 1973) to the individual leader. Thus, if the performance of an organisation is judged as strong, it becomes easier to make attributions about the success to individual leaders who can then justify significant rewards. In popular literature, the link of individual leader to success is the source of various leader heroes such as Jack Welch or Richard Branson. Of course, whether the opposite applies in times of failure, such as the recent GFC, is a moot point and there has been criticism of leaders and the failure to make them responsible for what went wrong (Board, 2010).

That individual leaders are central to leadership can be seen in the search for the particular features that make for good leaders, including the link to performance and success. Initially, the search focused on generic explanations of the concept and the possession of particular traits, even though it was not always possible to specify which of a large number of traits were appropriate. However, the view of leaders as special people who could be studied objectively to reveal an 'essence' of leadership was sustained and has continued into current times (Kakabadse and Kakabadse, 1999). Thus, post-war explanations focused on behaviours or styles of leadership, which could be varied according to the situation including the task and the capabilities of others, 'the followers'.

So from the late 1980s, the main preoccupation has been with the transformational qualities of leaders, those who can change an organisation, often in radical ways in order to adjust to competitive pressures brought about by such things as rapidly changing technologies and globalisation (Burns, 1978; Bennis, 1999). The transformational leader, we were led to believe, seeks to generate commitment and motivation and empower others with a vision. Often imbued with great charisma, these leaders served to transform 'others' who in turn followed this vision and wider organisational goals sometimes against their immediate self-interest (Kreitner *et al.*, 2002). More recently the qualities of emotional intelligence and ethical behaviour such as integrity and authenticity have been added to the list of competencies specified as desirable behaviour for leaders of organisations (Goleman *et al.*, 2002; Kalshoven *et al.*, 2011; Gardner *et al.*, 2005).

As a consequence of this initial preoccupation, it became necessary within organisations to acquire the tools to identify those who could become the leaders, and thus developed a focus on toolkits. There is of course a vast library of such resources available in a well-developed industry of leadership development suppliers. Most offer their versions of the 'essence' of leadership – the core factors or attributes distilled from research – and how particular approaches and sets of attributes, skills and knowledge are necessary for leaders. Within organisations, these have frequently been presented as frameworks of competences, which for nearly 30 years have been valued for their simple and clear purpose; they can provide a way of describing the behaviour of leaders that is needed for effective performance and provide the criteria for judgements about the achievement for purposes such as remuneration, development and the identification of talent and 'outstanding performers' (Boyatzis, 2008, p. 11). Competences therefore provide a simple argument which serves organisation performance. Competences specify attributes, skills and abilities that a jobholder needs to possess in order to carry out a particular role effectively (Miller *et al.*, 2001). Bolden and Gosling (2006, p. 148) give more detail in that a job competency can be defined as:

> 'an underlying characteristic of an individual that is causally related to effective or superior performance in a job' (Boyatzis, 1982: 21). Boyatzis identified 19 generic behavioural competencies associated with above average managerial performance, grouped into five clusters (goal and action management, leadership, human resource management, focus on others and directing subordinates).

There are some very well documented and long-standing problems with competences for leaders (see Gold *et al.*, 2010). One of the most searing critiques is the normative nature of competences that become an expression of an organisation's ideology, which has to be religiously observed (Finch-Lees *et al.*, 2005). Like other frameworks and typologies that are employed with reference to leader performance and development, competences can be seen as serving the function of an organisation's objectives, which are presented as neutral and objective. Further, Human Resource Management/Development (HRM/HRD) professionals could use the language of competences to show how their work aligns with organisational strategy. However, it is argued that a leader's work is more complex and changing than is implied by the 'simple representation' of competences (Bolden and Gosling, 2006). Recently it has been suggested that an uncritical acceptance of senior leaders' values which find expression in competences, was also a feature of the failure by HRM/HRD professionals to provide a counter to short-term and risky decisions that created the GFC (MacKenzie *et al.*, 2012).

Competences have also been used in relation to the idea of transformational leadership and one of the most well-known frameworks is the Multi-Factor Leadership Questionnaire (MLQ), based on the work of Avolio and Bass (2004). The questionnaire seeks to measure a leader against four dimensions: transformational, transactional, non-transactional (avoidant) and outcomes (effectiveness). A leader is rated against the elements of each dimension by up to 24 others who provide 360-degree feedback. It is interesting to note that the MLQ and the ideas of transformational or charismatic-transformational leadership have remained very popular in practice and research. For example, a recent review of academic papers on leadership theories showed that transformational and charismatic leadership theories represented 'the dominant forms of interest' (Dinh *et al.*, 2014, p. 39). However, also recently, van Knippenberg and Sitkin (2013) completed an assessment of the evidence for transformational leaders, and in particular, the link to organisation performance. They found so many problems with the basic understanding of the idea of charismatic transformation leadership, its measure and use, that they suggested abandoning the approach and starting again.

. . . and leadership

So much of the attention to leaders seems to assume a 'heroic' and 'great man' status that binds us to the Leader = Leadership identity. However, for quite some time this identity has been challenged. For example, as long ago as 1978, Burns argued that 'If we know all too much about our leaders, we know far too little about leadership. We fail to grasp the essence of leadership that is relevant to the modern age' (p. 1). In 1999, Senge suggested, 'There's a snowball's chance in hell of redefining leadership in this day and age' (p. 81). Since these comments were made, there have been doubts about the view that an 'essence of leadership' can be identified (Lawler, 2005). To appreciate this quandary, try the following question, posed in Kelly (2014, p. 913):

> Based on your knowledge of your own or any other organisation, if you walked in the front entrance – 'where is the leadership?'

The question might be confusing but stay with it for a moment, ask some colleagues and you might find some interesting responses (we would be happy to hear these, so please send them to us).

Commentators like Kelly argue that the word 'leadership' is open to so many views and definitions, that 'it becomes increasingly difficult to find any essential meaning in the term leadership at all' (2014, p. 918). Our own view is that if you know where to look and how to look, you can find leadership but it will be different from the static one-person notion and requires an understanding of what is happening in practice, as it happens. This reveals what we call the Leader's Conundrum.

Try the network mapping exercise in Box 6.1.

Box 6.1 Network mapping exercise

1. Place a sheet of A4 paper on a table, landscaped.
2. Place yourself as matchstick person in the centre of the page – this is where you are in your work practice situation.
3. Find at least one other person who depends on your work to do theirs; you try to influence their performance, but they depend on you. (Only one other person needs to be identified – there are likely to be others that you influence.) Draw that person to the right of you, with an arrow to show the flow of influence.
4. Now repeat the process to the left of you, but identifying one other person on whom you depend to do your work, thus influencing you. Draw an arrow to show this flow of influence. (Of course, there may be others on whom you depend.)
5. You have now identified a sequential view of leadership based on influence and dependence. It may be working well or not, but that is for you to judge.

6. Now, find a person who depends on you but you also depend on them. Draw this person below you with arrows going in both directions. There is a shared leadership practice here, and it is based on interdependence because it could not be completed without recognition of the mutuality and the need for collaboration. Again, you might have several such relationships, and the quality of the collaboration may vary between them.
7. Finally, we can repeat the interdependence idea, but with more than one other person. This is between at least three people, but there could easily be more who are all interdependent with each other. This can be your team or department. Draw this above you, but with dual-headed arrows going in all directions. Crucially, everyone you involve has a part of the practice and exerts influence on others but in return has to respond to the influence of others. It becomes a collective practice.

If you follow the stages of the exercise, you will be able to consider various units of dependent and interdependent practices that are essential for any organisation. If you use your imagination, you will also become aware of the way the pattern you identify is repeated throughout an organisation of any size and location. One way of considering the patterns is by seeing leadership as part of the process of influence and dependence. You might also consider whether the working of influence is contributing to the organisation purpose, direction and achievement of outcome measures – or not. That is, leadership that is considered in this collective mode of understanding, can be more or less aligned with organisational aims. A key point starts to emerge; how can those who are appointed as leaders and who are responsible for the achievement of organisational outcomes become aware of and begin to see the patterns of dependencies and interdependencies in daily practice that form leadership in the organisation? Can leaders embrace the conundrum or fall victim to the paradox of distortion?

One response is to begin to understand recent ideas and theories that consider leadership in more collective terms. For example, Raelin (2011) presents the idea of leaderful practice based on people working collectively together such that everyone has some role in influencing and leading. The group, as Raelin suggests, is not 'leaderless', it is '*leaderful*' (italics in original, p. 203). This is not difficult to understand, although as Raelin highlights, it is 'based on a democratic ideology' and requires an approach to leadership development based on co-creation and dialogue.

Another response is to see a number of varied patterns where individuals are contrasted against groups and collectives in a mix of leadership configurations (Gronn, 2009). This recognises that numbers involved in leadership can vary from single individuals through to all those engaged in the enterprise and beyond, regardless of their position in the hierarchy. Interest moves from one person to all kinds of practices and situations where influence is exerted. This can include pairs working together or teams and groups but also networks of practitioners. In all such work, distributed leadership is occurring, considered as the working of influence within a context, underpinned by culture and history (Spillane, 2006).

In recent years, there has been growing interest in the idea and practice of distributed leadership and, we suggest, an understanding of the evidence can help leaders face the conundrum. Bolden (2011) provides a very useful overview of the various approaches but if you refer back to your diagram of dependent and interdependent practices, you might be able to see what you have found matches the patterns of distributed leadership found by Spillane (2006), shown in Box 6.2.

Box 6.2 Patterns of distributed leadership (source: Spillane, 2006, p. 60)

- **Collaborated distribution**: where two or more individuals work together in time and place to execute the same leadership routine.
- **Collective distribution**: where two or more individuals work separately but interdependently to enact a leadership routine.
- **Coordinated distribution**: where two or more individuals work in sequence in order to complete a leadership routine.

For leaders to embrace their conundrum, they need to see leadership as a social process composed of complex relationships which highlight leadership as a process that is contextualised, emergent, connected to cultural and historical influences and always in a process of change and flux (Uhl-Bien, 2006) – one that is never easy to pin down. In the next section, we will explore this further by considering one organisation during a period of intense and radical change. To help us, we will employ Wittgenstein's (1969) metaphor of a river to illustrate the connection of culture and the leadership process. The river and the river-bed serve to highlight that amidst the daily 'flows and eddies' of life, there is a bedrock present that shapes the speed, depth and direction of thoughts and actions in the context of organisational life. The shared river-bank provides a certain degree of security of direction and this allows individuals to engage in a dialogue that at least has some bounds and direction. But nothing is absolutely fixed – the river-bed can move and in so doing, give rise to confusion and misunderstanding as a new course is set.

If we take an orthodox, individualistic view of leadership, the organisational 'heroic' leader might be seen as the grand geologist who maps out the course of the river, builds its banks and focuses on its ultimate destination – its outlet to the wider sea – before letting the sluice gates open and flooding the river-bed with staff whose direction is dictated by those banks. The geological paradox, though, is: which comes first – the river or the river-banks? Arguably they are created simultaneously. We know that the course of rivers is the result of a dynamic interaction between water and earth and is influenced also by other factors, the nature of the local geology, the local climate and weather, etc. At times the river may be in spate, destroying old banks and forming a new course. At other times or at other stages of the river's progress, the ground may be impervious to the water's action and the course of the river remains unaltered, the banks regulating and controlling the turbulence in the water. Wittgenstein describes this interaction or paradox in this way:

> And the bank of the river consists partly of hard rock, subject to no alteration or only to an imperceptible one, partly of sand, which now in one place now in another gets washed away, or deposited.
>
> *(Wittgenstein, 1969, p. 99)*

To the naive observer's eye, the course of river is permanent, to the geologist's eye, it is evidencing one stage of development. To the fish in the river or the kayaker, it demonstrates an element of permanence but both experience the river's inconsistencies, its turbulent and wild spots, its areas of calm. And indeed there is much that goes on beneath the surface of the river which is not visible to the external observer.

Arnswald's (2002) view of this metaphor is that systems of forces operate through a particular structure and influence our understanding of the world. The river-bed provides this structure but the forces which operate on, in and through it are complex and dynamic. The river-bed and river-banks both affect the river's inhabitants directly and indirectly. We will now go on to consider one particular, anonymised organisation using our river-banks metaphor. Whilst reading this, you might find it fruitful to think about your own organisational experience and to consider questions such as:

- How would you describe the 'river' of your own organisation?
- How immutable are its banks: how often does it overflow its course (or dry up?); who causes the major 'splashes' and what is the result?
- To what extent do people shape the river and to what extent are they carried along or swept away by it?
- How would different people describe their experience of the river?

The case

We studied a large commercial organisation to consider a radical change by senior managers and the establishment of a 'new organisation' with a key element of its new strategy becoming more innovative in order to improve competitiveness. However, evidence from the quarterly survey of employees indicated some dissonance between the declaration of the 'new organisation' and employees' experience of it! There were indications of alienation and detachment both from the change process and from the resultant 'new organisation'. This was evidenced by the expression of cynicism regarding future success, which matched experiences of previous change initiatives. The river as charted on the new organisational map did not feel to be running in the declared direction. Indeed employees felt it was following a different course from that charted and were sceptical about the actual destination.

As part of our exploration of the impact of this change, we organised two workshops, involving 24 participants from different parts of the UK. Our aim was to examine their views on the 'new organisation' and their interpretations of how leadership was operating. One of the interesting features of our workshop process was that it allowed those attending to reflect on the sources of influence where they worked. Paradoxically, while they were expecting this influence to belong to those in higher positions as appointed leaders, they were failing to acknowledge their own potential for exerting influence with others.

Our findings revealed some key themes that suggested misalignment between strategic intention and actual experience. People were not confused about where they were on the river but felt distant and detached from the river's geological foundations. Leaders were faced with the conundrum in three particular ways:

Firstly, there was evidence of both trust and distrust in leaders at all levels. These particular features of trust were highlighted:

- Trust was seen as a two-way process but in practice led to diverse results – positive where there were high levels of trust but negative where distrust occurred. Following our metaphor, where the banks of the river were not solid, the river diverged and minor backwaters developed, or stronger subsidiary flows developed in other directions.
- Where participants had confidence both in their leaders and their own ability to influence they could experience a feeling of mutual trust, with a belief that the words of leaders matched their deeds. Metaphorically, the river-banks were robust and the flow was directed and purposeful.
- Distrust, unease and scepticism occurred where there was a mismatch between leaders' words and actions: a variety of divergent flows and eddies developed.

Secondly, because of the uncertainty resulting from the initiation of the 'new organisation' employees paid close attention to the words and actions of their leaders. While participants were broadly positive about the new strategy and wanted it to work, doubts and scepticism were still apparent and evidence of any significant impact of the change was still felt to be lacking. Again, such feelings were reinforced by previous experiences they had had of organisational changes. In such situations, staff used the 'track record' of past changes as a guide to expectations. The river-bank as history was asserting itself and strongly countering any efforts to change course.

Thirdly, participants pointed to the length of time the process took to get new ideas accepted – broad, mid-stream pools developed, where the river's pace appeared to be sluggish. Decision-making was slow, risk aversion increased, contrary to the stated aim of being more innovative, and employees became passive followers rather than leaders. The culture reinforced cost reduction and short-termism, in turn affecting decision-making. There was little sign of innovation and participants felt that local leaders remained within their personal 'comfort zones' preventing any significant progress being made.

Fourthly, and again paradoxically, distrust did not extend as far as the CEO. Indeed, he was treated with a degree of reverence, seen as being able to 'define the new organisation', to have the passion to inspire staff to 'kiss the badge' and to continue the 'courageous' journey. There was clear evidence of a significant amount of trust present in the CEO even though some participants had not met him. Thus 'I hope you exist though I've not seen you' was followed by further expressions of faith, as it were, in the exhortation for the CEO to 'find the believers and spread the message' and that he should 'be visible and be seen'. The heroic expectations placed on the CEO were reinforced by the view that *he* was in control and the strategy and direction were defined by *him*, and that the senior managers *did not play* an active part in this – they simply had to 'go with the flow'. To this extent river-building was seen to be a singular, once and for all activity rather than a continuous, dynamic and at times iterative process.

These findings on the part played by the CEO match traditional views on how those appointed to leader roles are meant to behave and what duties should be enacted. As a relatively new CEO, rather than accepting the previous course of the river, from the past, the staff were wanting to see a fresh direction to be created, one in which pride and passion are given prominence. The reverence with which staff flavoured their comments suggests a reliance on the heroic aspects of a CEO, as someone who can rescue an organisation by articulating a vision of the future together with a sense of direction whilst holding others to account for their performance. This kind of articulation resonates well with images of leaders as practical authors (Holman and Thorpe, 2003) where a meaningful landscape of possibilities becomes the message and others come into this landscape to create the new reality, or in this case, the new organisation. However, and this shows the importance of appreciating the working of the conundrum, a single articulation is insufficient, especially when participants expect their CEO to be more visible to staff in the organisation. In some of their responses, staff noted they were unsure as to whether this persona actually existed! This is a point we will develop in the next section.

In contrast with the expectations for the CEO, there seemed to be a 'business as usual' approach to life and the change for the 'new organisation'. The 'How' of implementation was, from this research, being hindered by the history of the organisation in terms of the way it conducted its business – a form of organisational inertia or evidence that the traditional course and flow of the river remained unaltered and were perceived to be unalterable and inevitable. Turbulence might be introduced but it was only temporary and did not disturb the overall flow in the longer term, in much the same way as throwing a series of rocks in the river might create a big splash but are unlikely to have any lasting impact. We can see how culture forms an important part of the river metaphor here. The organisation's history pointed to low levels of 'self-confidence' and 'self-belief' among local leaders with decision-making being a laboured process and decisions themselves often altered – perhaps seen as occasional stones cast into the river. Viewed as 'bureaucratic, slow and stifling', 'lacking in direction', with managers and leaders 'out of the same mould', the organisation was seen to have 'no champions of change' and the organisation had a history of treating staff 'as children' and so consequently, they 'behaved like children'.

These rather damning features of the organisation were very much in evidence to the staff, from their position on one side of the riverbank but appeared to be hidden from the CEO and other leaders.

They, it appeared, were working on the surface of the river, whilst beneath there was considerable tumult as a consequence, the words and actions became distorted and contradictions emerged. At this point we suggest another image from Wittgenstein (1980), which relates to this notion of the 'whole hurly-burly' (p. 629). This refers to the complex pattern of the various forms of life that form the basis and ongoing energy for culture and values within an organisation. This offers for leaders the potential that whatever the certainty and accuracy achieved in the construction of plans and strategies, there is always a background to this work in the 'bustle' of everyday life (1980, p. 625) as people at work respond to the various initiatives and propositions are made. A principal component to this background is the conversations between people made where and while they work within the traditions and history of the organisation but brought to life in the present through stories told and enacted (Ford *et al.*, 2002). It is in such circumstances from the cacophony of voices that local influence is exerted, which in turn can institutionalise an accepted understanding of change (Phillips *et al.*, 2004). This we believe forms the basis for distributed leadership to take hold and is likely to lie beyond the grasp of many leaders (Gronn, 2000).

Reflections on the case

Given the limitations on our view from the river-banks, some way downstream – 24 participants from of over 10,000 staff does not constitute a comprehensive picture or route map (intended or emerging . . .) of the river but we could at least discern some formations and flows. Those in formal leader positions were seen as followers rather than shapers, promotion was on the basis of having served their time and there was a general 'lack of trust' within the organisation. The history suggested being slow to respond to changes in the market and that 'self-interest would prevail', and that this constrained development. Despite reverence for the CEO and a desire for him to set the vision, there was a general lack of clarity regarding strategic direction through 'filtering', becoming 'stuck' or being 'blocked'. Quite a conundrum for the leader.

There are no quick fixes for appointed leaders but the first move has to be to accept and embrace the conundrum and recognise they cannot know it all, even if others expect them to – another paradox. One starting point is nicely captured by a well-known quotation from Ludwig Wittgenstein:

> A picture held us captive. And we could not get outside it, for it lay in our language and language seemed to repeat it to us inexorably.
>
> *(Wittgenstein, 2001, p. 115)*

In our context the picture we are using is cartographical and the image of the leader is as someone who charts the river's course. Not only does the leader need to have a clear view of the river's intended course (perhaps canal-builder might be an easier derivation of the metaphor here . . .) but s/he also needs to know in practice, how is the course faring, is it altering or is all as intended? In our view, one of the most challenging fearful difficulties for appointed leaders is how they come to rely on images (and metaphors) and language about the business that have been filtered and cleaned for their consumption. One notable example of this is the way US President Richard Nixon's 'advisory group' filtered and regulated information from the wider world and influenced his perspective of his own role, with 'Watergate' as the consequence (see Raven, 1998). This is not surprising since, and this depends on the size and spread of the organisation as well as the outsiders who watch the business, it is the job of support staff such as Finance, HR and others to ensure that messy and dirty pictures do not reach the top. We had first-hand experience of this effect when we presented our findings to the leaders of the organisation in the case above. We prepared a report from our workshops with 24 staff, containing their views as reported to us. Of course, there was much critique of what was happening in their 'new' organisation. We found that this would not be considered acceptable by the leaders, according to the Communications Director, so we re-wrote it and tried to present a less critical version. It was rejected again. The third version, which was accepted, was much reduced with little critique.

Appointed leaders need other images to provide a way of avoiding the conundrum and falling victim to the paradox of distortion. To help form such an image we turn to an example reported in the

Guardian on 9 April 2002 which you can still find online at www.guardian.co.uk/society/2002/apr/09/localgovernment.education.

It tells the story of how Birmingham Education Authority moved from a very poor position in the early 1990s to one of great improvement by 2002. Central to this improvement was the work of the Chief Education Officer, Tim Brighouse. At the time, Brighouse had a reputation that made him unpopular within government circles, although he was much admired in the education world. The article shows how he sought to energise everyone involved in Birmingham schools. Importantly, he attributed much of the change not to himself but to the collaborative work with others. Once you have read the article, consider how his version of what happened contrasts with the 'heroic' image of the leader presented by the report. For example, he deflects the attention on him and prefers instead to point to the collective effort – 'We have been very, very focused' and 'We set out always to improve'. What is also important is how he dealt with the conundrum he faced by visiting both sides of the river-bank as part of the journey by building bridges between the banks.

Whether a myth or real, what comes through to us is that as an appointed leader, Brighouse was not held captive by a fixed and cleaned picture of life in the schools, he got out of his office, listened to others, attending to details and explaining what would happen – words and deeds synchronised. He helped plan and shape the course of the river, bearing in mind the local geology (legislative and resource framework), the current flow through existing river-banks and river-bed (local organisational and political contexts) and the current depth, eddies, deposits (organisational and professional cultures). No wonder Brighouse said it was 99 per cent hard work but this is the energy that others needed to see so they could do it too.

Having set the intended direction of the river, and you can see, this was not a quick-fix effort, but once it was set, as the author of the message, the actions of the leader allowed for continuous repetition not just for the sake of clarity but to build with others, practically, the story of what was happening and how. This allowed the spread of good stories by the leader but also many others, which celebrated success, highlighting Weick's (1996) advice on the contribution of stories to organisational sensemaking. What is also striking about the way the story is told is attention given to 'energy'. Notice the question: 'Are we not energy creators in this place?'

Conclusion

In this chapter, our argument is that because appointed leaders face a conundrum which results in a paradox of distortion caused by the way the everyday practice of leadership is distributed, it becomes incumbent on appointed leaders to see themselves as initiators, inspirational or otherwise, who set out to work with the energy of others so that they might, in turn, add to the flow of energy. However, the flow of energy will, to a strong degree, feed local self-organising leadership that is distributed and affected by interests in local settings (see Tesone, 2000). Therefore an appointed leader, and hopefully others, needs to argue for the direction they seek to pursue. They need to decide whether to direct the river or to go with its flow. More accurately and rather than 'either/or', they need to decide the extent to which they can direct the river and the extent to which they are directed by it. Their own potential within this dynamic, to influence its flow, might be more considerable when they realise their inability to directly 'control' what happens in the organisation. Like the river, it is an unending process but in engaging with the organisation's dynamics – its strategy, culture and people – they will come to work with the energy of a leadership that is made meaningful through collective endeavour of people relating to one another at work (Uhl-Bien, 2006).

Questions for reflection and discussion

1. Think of an organisation in which you work, have worked, or know, and consider the following questions:

    a. When does the river metaphor fit? Where doesn't it fit, and why?
    b. Where is the organisation flowing and where is it stuck? What could be done that might help to open up any bottlenecks?
    c. Does the river's course feel fixed or is its course changing and if so how? What might help it move to a better course?
    d. How well is the leaders' description of the organisation's course understood? Is there just one story being told, by a single leader, or multiple stories from different leaders?

e. How much trust is there that the organisation can or will get there? What is helping to build trust within the organisation and what might be limiting trust within the organisation?
f. How energised are the staff? What limits their energy? What changes in leadership style/behaviours might help them feel more energised?

2. Imagine yourself as the CEO mentioned in the case study in this chapter.

   a. How would it feel to be faced by the conundrum whereby you are simultaneously expected to articulate a clear vision of the future whilst also recognising that this vision needs to be co-produced with followers in order to create a sense of shared ownership and commitment?
   b. How would you go about creating and articulating this vision and direction given the organisational context and the expectations placed upon you in your role?
   c. What key indicators and/or milestones would you need to identify, monitor and evaluate to ensure you, and the organisation, were on track?

3. Read the story about Tim Brighouse and the Birmingham Education Authority at: www.guardian.co.uk/society/2002/apr/09/localgovernment.education.

   a. How many thank you notes did Brighouse send?
   b. How much was inspiration and how much was hard work?
   c. To what extent do you believe the account written in this article – are there any parts of the story that are missing and/or perspectives that are not considered?
   d. Do you think it is reasonable to attribute so much of the success of this change process to Brighouse? Who/what else might have contributed to these outcomes?

Recommended reading

Bolden, R. and Gosling, J. 2006. Leadership Competencies: Time to Change the Tune? *Leadership* 2(2): 147–163.

Ford, J., Ford, L. and McNamara, R. 2002. Resistance and the Background Conversations of Change. *Journal of Organizational Change Management* 15(2): 105–121.

Gold, J., Thorpe, R. and Mumford, A. (eds) (2010) *Gower Handbook of Leadership and Management Development* (5th Edition). Aldershot: Gower.

Lawler, J. 2005. The 'Essence' of Leadership? Existentialism and Leadership. *Leadership* 1(2): 215–231.

Uhl-Bien, M. 2006. Relational Leadership Theory: Exploring the Social Processes of Leadership and Organizing. *The Leadership Quarterly* 17: 654–676.

References

Alvessson, M. and Spicer, A. 2012. Critical Leadership Studies: The Case for Critical Performativity. *Human Relations* 65(3): 367–390.

Arnswald, U. 2002. On the Certainty of Uncertainty: Language Games and Forms of Life in Gadamer and Wittgenstein, in Malpas, J., Arnswald, U. and Kertscher, J. (eds), *Gadamer's Century: Essays in Honor of Hans-Georg Gadamer*. Massachusetts, MIT: 25–44.

Avolio, B. and Bass, B. 2004. *Multifactor Leadership Questionnaire: Manual and Sampler Set*. Redwood City, CA: Mind Garden.

Bass, B. 1985. *Leadership and Performance Beyond Expectations*. New York, NY: Free Press.

Bennis, W. 1999. Exemplary Leadership Is Impossible Without Full Inclusion, Initiatives and Cooperation of Followers. *Organizational Dynamics* 28(1): 71–80.

Board, D. 2010. Leadership: The Ghost at the Trillion Dollar Crash? *European Management Journal* 28: 269–277.

Bolden, R. 2011. Distributed Leadership in Organizations: A Review of Theory and Research. *International Journal of Management Reviews* 13: 251–269.

Bolden, R. and Gosling, J. 2006. Leadership Competencies: Time to Change the Tune? *Leadership* 2(2): 147–163.

Bolden, R., Hawkins, B., Gosling, J. and Taylor, S. 2011. *Exploring Leadership: Individual, Organizational and Societal Perspectives*. Oxford: Oxford University Press.

Boyatzis, R.E. 2008. Competencies in the 21st Century. *Journal of Management Development* 27(1): 5–12.

Burns, J.M. 1978. *Leadership*. New York, NY: Harper & Row.

Dinh, J., Lord, R.G., Gardner, W., Meuser, J.D., Liden, R. and Hu, J. 2014. Leadership Theory and Research in the New Millennium: Current Theoretical Trends and Changing Perspectives. *The Leadership Quarterly* 25: 36–62.

Finch-Lees, T., Mabey, C. and Liefooghe, A. 2005. In the Name of Capability: A Critical Discursive Evaluation of Competency-Based Management Development. *Human Relations* 58(9): 1185–1222.

Ford, J., Ford, L. and McNamara, R. 2002. Resistance and the Background Conversations of Change. *Journal of Organizational Change Management* 15(2): 105–121.

Gardner, W.L., Avolio, B.J., Luthans, F., May, D.R. and Walumbwa, F.O. 2005. 'Can You See the Real Me?' A Self Based Model of Authentic Leader and Follower Development. *Leadership Quarterly* 16: 343–372.

Gold, J., Thorpe, R. and Mumford, A. 2010. *Leadership and Management Development*. London: Chartered Institute of Personnel and Development.

Goleman, D., Boyatzis, R. and McKee, A. 2002. *Primal Leadership: Realizing the Power of Emotional Intelligence*. Cambridge, MA: HBR Press.

Gronn, P. 2000. Distributed Properties: A New Architecture for Leadership. *Educational Management Administration & Leadership* 28: 317–338.

Gronn, P. 2009. Leadership Configurations. *Leadership* 5(3): 381–394.

Holman, D. and Thorpe, R. (eds) 2003. *Management and Language*. London: Sage Publications.

Hunt, J.G. 1999. Transformational/Charismatic Leadership's Transformation of the Field: A Historical Essay. *Leadership Quarterly* 10: 129–144.

Kakabadse, A. and Kakabadse, N. 1999. *Essence of Leadership*. London: International Thomson.

Kalshoven, K., Den Hartog, D. and De Hoogh, A. 2011. Ethical Leadership at Work Questionnaire (ELW): Development and Validation of a Multidimensional Measure. *The Leadership Quarterly* 22(1): 51–69.

Kelley, H.H. 1973. The Processes of Causal Attribution. *American Psychologist* 28: 107–128.

Kelly, S. 2014. Towards a Negative Ontology of Leadership. *Human Relations* 67(8): 905–922.

van Knippenberg, D.V. and Sitkin, S.B. 2013. A Critical Assessment of Charismatic—Transformational Leadership Research: Back to the Drawing Board? *The Academy of Management Annals* 7(1): 1–60.

Kreitner, R., Kinicki, A. and Buelens, M. 2002. *Organizational Behavior*. Toronto, ON: McGraw-Hill.

Lawler, J. 2005. The 'Essence' of Leadership? Existentialism and Leadership. *Leadership* 1(2): 215–231.

MacKenzie, C., Garavan, T. and Carberry, R. 2012. Through the Looking Glass: Challenges for Human Resource Development (HRD) Post the Global Financial Crisis – Business as Usual? *Human Resource Development International* 15: 353–364.

Miller, L., Rankin, N. and Neathey, F. 2001. *Competency Frameworks in UK Organizations*. London: CIPD.

Phillips, N., Lawrence, T.B. and Hardy, N. 2004. Discourse and Institutions. *Academy of Management Review* 29(4): 635–652.

Raelin, J. 2011. From Leadership-as-Practice to Leaderful Practice. *Leadership* 7(1): 195–211.

Raven, B.H. 1998. Groupthink, Bay of Pigs, and Watergate Reconsidered. *Organizational Behavior and Human Decision Processes* 73(2/3): 352–361.

Senge, P. 1999. The Gurus Speak (panel discussion): Complexity and Organizations. *Emergence* 1(1): 73–91.

Spillane, J.P. 2006. *Distributed Leadership*. San Francisco, CA: Jossey-Bass.

Tesone, D. 2000. Leadership and Motivating Missions: A Model for Organizations from Science Literature. *Journal of Leadership & Organizational Studies* 7(1): 60–69.

Uhl-Bien, M. 2006. Relational Leadership Theory: Exploring the Social Processes of Leadership and Organizing. *The Leadership Quarterly* 17: 654–676.

Weick, K.E. 1996. *Sensemaking in Organizations*. Newbury Park, CA: Sage.

Wittgenstein, L. 1969. *On Certainty*. New York, NY: Harper.

Wittgenstein, L. 1980. *Remarks on the Philosophy of Psychology*, vol 2. Oxford: Blackwell.

Wittgenstein, L. 2001 [1953]. *Philosophical Investigations*, G. Anscombe and R. Rhees (eds), G. Anscombe (trans.). Oxford: Blackwell.

7

LEADERSHIP AND THE PARADOXES OF AUTHENTICITY

Inmaculada Adarves-Yorno

In this chapter Immaculada Adarves-Yorno brings to life the paradoxes of authenticity, from the conceptual to the contextual, and from matters of identity to the journey to authenticity itself. You will become familiar with many of the difficulties inherent in authenticity and be better equipped to develop your own form of authentic leadership. Blending an in-depth understanding of psychology and her practical experience of working within organisations and as a consultant and advisor to CEOs, she applies a broad range of theory and provides pointers to your own development.

In 2003 Bill George, former CEO of Medtronic plc, argued that, 'due to the current crisis, complexities and challenges facing our society and organizations nowadays we need from a new type of leadership—the authentic leader'. Following that line of thought, the *Harvard Business Review* published an article by Goffee and Jones in which the authors noted that 'leadership demands the expression of an authentic self' (Goffee and Jones, 2005). A decade later 'authenticity has become the gold standard for leaders' (Ibarra, 2015). On the surface, authentic leadership represents an ideal for leaders to aspire to. But unfortunately a simplistic understanding of authenticity can hinder a leader's development (Ibarra, 2015).

This chapter exposes some of the complexities and nuances of authentic leadership by capturing some of the 'true' and paradoxical aspects of authenticity. This nuanced picture is informed by (a) the work of leadership scholars combined with (b) my background of 20 years studying and working in psychology, (c) my experience as a CEO advisor and HR manager, (d) my work and reflections as a leadership developer and coach, (e) my academic theoretical understanding and (f) my own internal work aiming to become an authentic leader.

Many of the common understandings and scholarly approaches to authenticity revolve around a coherent picture of the authentic leader. Can authentic leaders be anything other than consistent and congruent? A simplistic view of authentic leadership would argue *No*. Yet a deeper understanding of authentic leadership requires that we comprehend its complexity. Accordingly, this chapter presents and comments on four paradoxes. A visual way of organising these paradoxes is by presenting them along two dimensions: horizontal and vertical. On the horizontal we find three paradoxes of breadth: (a) *the conceptual paradox* – aspiring to fit within the definition of authentic leadership can distance yourself from your authenticity, (b) *the contextual paradox* – in some contexts being authentic to your *Self* can be perceived as anything but authentic, and (c) *the identity paradox* – we may be authentic to different and contradictory selves. On the vertical dimension we find the *paradox of depth* in which aspects of the self that are encountered at different levels may contradict each other. To end, this chapter offers a reflective exercise as a means of starting a self-discovery journey.

Paradoxes of breadth

Conceptual paradox

There are many definitions of authenticity and authentic leadership (for an overview see Gardner *et al.*, 2011). The present chapter focuses on two commonly used conceptualisations and it explores the paradoxes that emerge from them. *Authenticity* is defined *as knowing oneself and acting accordingly* (Harter, 2002; Endrissat *et al.*, 2007). In that sense, authenticity revolves around being true to your Self (Lid-Falkman, 2014). Another commonly used definition emerges from the Authentic Leadership Approach (Avolio and Gardner, 2005). According to this approach, authentic leaders are defined as those who

> are deeply aware of how they think and behave and are perceived by others as being aware of their own and others' values/moral perspectives, knowledge and strengths; aware of the context in which they operate; and who are confident, hopeful, optimistic, resilient and of high moral character.
>
> *(Avolio, Luthans* et al., *2004: 4, as cited in Avolio, Gardner* et al., *2004: 802, 803)*

The first paradox emerges from the authentic leadership conceptualisation itself. Leaders exhibiting high levels of authenticity (i.e. being true to themselves) do not always fit with Avolio and Gardner's definition. In fact, as Ladkin and Taylor (2010) noted, having positive psychological capabilities (such as confidence, hope, optimism) may be authentic for some leaders but not for others. Similarly, Wilson (2013) explains that even if authentic leaders are 'confident, hopeful, optimistic and resilient' on some occasions they are also uncertain, pessimistic and fragile on other occasions. Finally, Shamir and Eilam (2005) argued that authenticity per se does not necessarily need to be related to positive, ethical or moral behaviour. In fact, controversially there are those leaders who are authentic to dubious immoral values. Following the aforementioned presented reasoning, they too can be acting from a place of authenticity and on that basis could be considered authentic leaders – albeit not in ways we would like to encourage.

I first encountered this paradox when I started teaching authentic leadership. I used to explain the authentic leadership approach during the lecture and then invite the students to enter into a journey of authentic leadership development. Paradoxically, *some of my students needed to be inauthentic* (e.g. pretend to be optimistic) *to fit with the definition of an 'authentic leader'*. My students felt an inherent contradiction when they were invited to discover and enact their authentic self, but the Self that they discovered was in many instances far away from the definition postulated by Avolio and colleagues. Even if they were good leaders who were true to themselves they did not qualify formally as authentic leaders. To fit into the authentic leaders' 'box' these leaders needed to metaphorically hide and/or exaggerate some aspects of themselves. How authentic was that?

Paradox 1: Leaders may need to sacrifice their authenticity to fit within a definition of authentic leadership.

Contextual paradox

Followers' assessment of leaders' authenticity is context dependent (Fields, 2013). Some of the factors that impact on followers' evaluations are: (a) job role expectations, (b) past experience with leaders, (c) followers' implicit models of the characteristics associated with a good leader, and (d) the norms present within the culture of the organisational setting (Fields, 2013: 147). Therefore if a leader wants to be perceived as authentic, *being authentic is not enough*. Nyberg and Sveningsson (2014) argue that while authenticity is meant to make good leaders, these leaders also have to restrain their claimed authenticity depending on the context. Accordingly, while it has been argued that authentic leaders need to let others see their negative states such as uncertainty (Wilson, 2013), doing so maybe risky. In her *Harvard Business Review* paper, Ibarra (2015) described a general manager who, when she was promoted, said to her employees 'I want to do this job, but it's scary and I need your help'. This could be seen as an authentic disclosure of emotion and thus she could be seen as an authentic leader. Nonetheless, in the context where she was working, she lost credibility as the followers needed a confident leader to take charge. Paradoxically although authenticity is said to be required for good leadership (Nyberg and Sveningsson, 2014) the challenge of great leadership is to manage their authenticity (Goffee and Jones, 2005).

I experienced this paradox in action in my own work with the University of Exeter's One Planet MBA (OP MBA), co-founded and delivered with WWF International. This programme aims to develop a new generation of business leaders with a strong sustainability mindset – a 'One Planet' mindset (for more details see Jeanrenaud *et al.*, 2015). The module I was co-leading aimed to develop leaders differently and it placed a great emphasis on authentic leadership. Five years ago, during my first lecture I made sure that I portrayed myself as authentically as possible. I came to the lecture theatre as 'Inma', and I dressed to represent who I was, not as an academic but as a person (using informal clothes and wearing vibrant colours). It was a well-planned strategy. I didn't use any status cues as I wanted the students to connect with the 'real' Inma, not with the academic lecturer. Furthermore, I wanted students to know that during the module there was space to be themselves and for that wanted to role model the process by being 'myself'. To my surprise, the MBA students neither recognised nor appreciated my authenticity. Furthermore, some of them thought that I was a junior academic and they complained to the MBA director for sending someone who they considered to be an inexperienced lecturer. Using the aforementioned analysis by Fields (2013) my authenticity was at odds with their implicit models of what an MBA module leader should look like. Moreover, my 'true self', moving away from status, wearing informal clothes and displaying warmth of connection did not fit with the MBA culture. Intentions rooted in authenticity may in some contexts, like in this case, be misinterpreted. Aiming to act from an authentic place is an activity worth pursuing. But equally we should not ignore who we are leading and the context in which we are operating.

> **Paradox 2:** Being authentic does not directly enhance the perception of authenticity and can instead undermine one's leadership.

Identity paradox

Until now, this chapter has revolved around authenticity understood as encompassing a *true self* (George and Sims, 2007) with the assumption that there is *one* true self. However, Wilson (2013) argues that there are multifaceted and often contradictory aspects of our 'selves'. Yet, multiple identities have, to date, been largely overlooked in the area of authentic leadership (Gardiner, 2013). The multiplicity of identities is a key premise of a robust social psychological perspective. The social identity approach (encompassing social identity theory, SIT (Tajfel and Turner, 1979); and self-categorisation theory, SCT (Turner *et al.*, 1987)) argues that an individual's self is composed of a personal identity and as many social identities as meaningful groups the individual belongs to. The application and understanding of multiple identities has been proliferous in a wide range of areas including leadership. A well-documented series of empirical studies emphasise that, among other things, the effective leader needs to be 'one of us' (Haslam *et al.*, 2011). That is, the social identity approach would strongly argue that leaders do not only need to be authentic to 'I' but also they need to be authentic to 'us'.

This paradox is particularly pervasive when values and priorities from our different social identities conflict with each other (see social identity complexity; Roccas and Brewer, 2002). Let us imagine two leaders that occupy a senior management position. Externally in their team meeting leaders A and B appear really attentive to the followers' ideas and concerns. For example, when the followers share their concern about their precarious work–life balance Leaders A and B seem to share 'authentically' their own lack of balance and promise they will look into ways of improving the situation. Subsequently, in the senior management meeting it is announced that the organisation needs to become more productive and several options are discussed. In that meeting Leaders A and B commit their team to work under new challenging targets (increasing the precariousness of the work–life balance). Externally both leaders are behaving inconsistently and therefore could be judged as inauthentic. But, the potential internal processes underpinning their behaviour may be quite different. Let me give you a possible scenario. Leader A's behaviour stems from his personal identity and he identifies neither with his team nor with the management team. In psychological terms Leader A has his personal identity activated in both contexts and he is acting out of personal interest in both contexts. On the contrary, Leader B's behaviour stems from his high identification with both groups, which happen to have opposite values and priorities. That is, in his team meetings, his identity as 'one of the team' is activated and he is acting and talking from that place (really caring about the work–life balance of his employees). Nonetheless in the meeting with the senior management group his identity as 'one of the senior managers' is activated and he is acting and talking from that place (really believing that challenging targets are the solution needed). In psychological terms Leader B has contrasting and competing social identities activated in each context.

To illustrate further, let's look at a real life example. Sarah was the founder and CEO of a successful engineering company. She was considered a leader with a transparent style of communication, which elicited trust among employees. In her previous role Sarah was working as a graphic engineer for a multinational car manufacturer and she was heavily involved and committed to the trade union. Her identity, values and norms as a union rep were very strong and they determined her beliefs around work policies. However, as a CEO her identity revolved around different values regarding work policies. When I interviewed her she declared that the values of both identities were important to her but she acknowledged that sometimes these contradicted each other and therefore presented inner tensions. Through a series of conversations Sarah noted that when her CEO identity was salient she resisted the idea of hiring 'a woman who is about to have children'. On the contrary, when her union identity was activated she passionately declared that organisations need to hire women who are about to have children and that policies of flexible working and childcare need to be changed. If someone had listened to Sarah they may have found it difficult to accept that these two opposing arguments came from the same person. Consequently, the most common explanation of the incongruence would be to attribute the difference to her being inauthentic (to say the least). Through my conversations with her I can attest that it is not inauthenticity that lies at the root of the inconsistency but rather authenticity to competing identities.

> **Paradox 3**: An individual can be authentic to multiple, and in some cases contradictory, identities.

Dealing with the paradoxes of breadth

Within the authentic leadership approach the term 'authentic leader' came initially from the need to differentiate between transformational leaders and pseudo-transformational leaders (Avolio, 2011). A way of dealing with the *conceptual paradox* is by calling those leaders who fit within the definition given by Avolio and colleagues (2004) 'authentic transformational' and calling those who possess authenticity 'authentic leaders' (Kernis, 2003) meaning that they know themselves and are true to themselves (Harter, 2002). Making this conceptual distinction would mean that under leadership development, individuals could choose what type of authentic leader they want to become (i.e. feels more aligned with who they aspire to be). During their developmental journeys some leaders may choose to acquire high levels of optimism, hope, resilience, efficacy and moral character and therefore aspire to become an authentic transformational leader (as defined by Avolio, Gardner *et al.*, 2004).

Other leaders may want to become self-confident, genuine, reliable and trustworthy, which have been considered qualities of authentic leaders by Ilies *et al.* (2005). Yet others may choose to develop mindfulness, hope and compassion and in doing so they will be an example of a 'resonant leader' (as defined by Boyatzis and McKee, 2005).

A way of dealing with the *contextual and identity paradoxes* would be by engaging in what Ladkin and Taylor (2010) considered a critical aspect of authentic leadership – 'leaderly' choice. As part of that 'leaderly' choice individuals need to decide what aspects of oneself are appropriate to share. As Jean Tomlin (former HR manager of Marks & Spencer) explained, 'I want to be me, but I am channeling parts of me to context. What you get is a segment of me. It is not a fabrication or a façade – just the bits that are relevant for that situation' (Goffee and Jones, 2005). To make that 'leaderly' choice leaders need to identify what aspects are appropriate to express within the particular context as in the case of Jean. But also, which aspects resonate with the identity of the group they are leading (Gardner, 1995). For leaders to be perceived as authentic they need to relate to their followers (Taylor, 2013) and a successful authentic leader needs, among other things, to be perceived to be 'one of us' (Haslam *et al.*, 2011). In other words, to be an effective leader we need to represent and be authentic to 'us'. Therefore, while it is important to fully discover and embrace who we are, as leaders, we need to *lead others*, and we need to bear in mind who these others are and the context in which we are embedded.

When there is contradiction between the different identities within us, it is important to acknowledge that the activation of these identities depends on the social context (Turner *et al.*, 1987). By understanding the contexts that activate our different ranges of identity we are a step closer towards understanding ourselves. Some of us would like to minimise our inconsistency across contexts. However, doing so could make us be inauthentic to the activated identity that is operating at each point in time and would be forced and artificial. The tension between consistency and inconsistency of Self leads us to the paradox of depth.

The paradox of depth

Authenticity is shaped by social identities and the context but it also varies depending on the depth in which we engage our 'inner conversations'.

That is, as we enhance our awareness we uncover different levels of the Self, which may resurface tensions and contradictions.

An Authentic Leadership course provided by a prestigious and well-established Institute (Authentic Leadership in Action Institute, ALIA) started with the invitation 'let's be confused together'. And indeed to start with that provocation confused me. My preconceived assumptions let me expect some clarity and guidance. In due time, I realised that I was getting clarity and guidance on how to go deeper into myself and that when you go deep enough you encounter confusion. I then experienced that it is only through a certain level of accepted confusion that we can embark on truly deep authentic leadership development. One of the useful tools to navigate those dark waters of confusion is mindfulness. In simple terms, mindfulness is about being aware of what is happening while it is happening (Boyatzis and McKee, 2005: 2). But importantly, that form of awareness needs to be non-judgemental (Epstein, 1999). This kind of attention nurtures greater awareness, clarity and acceptance of present moment reality (Kabat-Zinn, 2011). But it is not just restricted to our inner experience. In fact, mindfulness is defined as the capacity to be fully aware of all that one experiences inside the self as well as to pay full attention to what is happening around (Boyatzis and McKee, 2005: 2). Judy Johansen, president and CEO, sees mindfulness as 'a way of life and a necessary baseline for success as a leader of a complex business' (Boyatzis and McKee, 2005: 2).

In 2013 I conducted a series of interviews and focus groups with members of ALIA, the aforementioned Institute, to explore the extent to which in-depth authentic communication with oneself (mindfulness) changed the notion of authenticity. The sample was composed of ALIA participants (in this case mindfulness beginners) and ALIA faculty (senior consultants and leadership developers who have decades of experience of mindfulness practice). The findings of this research allowed me to capture the paradox of 'depth'. For ALIA participants, authenticity was about congruency, alignment, coherence and resonance (reflecting an understanding of authenticity similar to mainstream approaches to authentic leadership as outlined earlier in this chapter). The opposite picture, however, emerged in the interviews and focus groups with faculty members. Those faculty members who have gone deeper in terms of self-awareness talked about fluidity and continuous change. Paradoxically, at a deeper level congruency across times was not highlighted but instead it was congruency with what was happening moment by moment, including incongruence itself. Accordingly, for ALIA faculty being aware of their own moments of inauthenticity was the gateway towards authenticity (for more details see Adarves-Yorno, 2013). For them the main emphasis was on acceptance of 'what is actually happening' even if that meant dissonance and incoherence.

> **Paradox 4**: At one level authenticity is experienced as congruency and coherence. At a deeper level authenticity is experienced as acceptance of *what is* including fluidity and inauthenticity.

To understand further this paradox it is important that we first comprehend *the illusion of congruence* and the *reality of disconnection*.

My experience working with leaders and aspiring leaders is that due to their lack of time and cognitive resources they tend to create a narrative that enhances their sense of congruence with themselves. However, in truth that narrative and the attachment to that narrative may be distancing them from reality itself. I used to work in a small company as both CEO advisor and HR manager. In that company I witnessed how the reality that the CEO had in her mind was in many instances quite different to that of the employees. But how could divergent realities co-exist in a small organisation? To address this question, let's uncover the underlying process of the 'disconnection to reality'. In the *Neuroscience of Change*, Kelly McGonigal (2012) explained how our mind in its default state does four things: (a) *time travel*: remembering things from the past, planning or imagining things from the future; (b) engages in *inner commentary*, that is judges and comments on what happens around, 'this is bad', 'this could be better', 'this is wonderful'; (c) engages in *self-referential processes*, that is, it selects bits of information in order to define the Self (e.g. 'I have spent two hours in that meeting listening patiently, because I am the kind of person who attends to everyone's views'); and (d) engages into *social cognition*, that is we judge and label others – 'he is kind', 'she is aggressive', 'he is competitive'.

Planning for the future and judging the environment, ourselves and others gives us a (false) sense of knowing 'in the future I am going to do X because the environment is Z, my colleagues are W and I am the type of person who does Y'. When a group of people is functioning from a place of judging and labelling, rather than being fully present and aware, the reality that is perceived by each of them can be quite different. This is shaped by, among other things, their underlying beliefs and self-images. Let me give you an example. Three years ago in a conversation with someone the person told me: 'Inma, you just don't see yourself.' My internal reaction was: 'How dare he? He is the one who does not see himself' (I judged him, social cognition). Then, I internally undermined his comment using some self-referential processes: 'I have been working on developing my self-awareness for a long time and I am a person who is very self-aware.' Following my perception that he was the one who was mistaken and assuming that there was no point in talking anymore I terminated the conversation. Later on that day I managed to have some detachment from the self-image of 'I am an aware person'. That detachment gave me space to see reality more clearly and then I realised that in fact he was right, I was not 'seeing myself'. Paradoxically, my attachment to the *self-image* that I was *self-aware* was in fact a *barrier to my own self-awareness*.

If leaders define themselves as 'authentic', in the sense that they are always congruent with their values, it is quite likely that they may become attached to that self-image. In that case, it is likely that their mind will disregard the instances in which they behave incongruently with those values. In that sense they will only stay on the surface 'pretending' to be authentic. Detachment and willingness to embrace our own incongruencies and incoherences are needed to embrace a deeper sense of fluid authenticity.

Conclusion

Aiming to fit into a prescribed definition of authentic leadership may distance leaders from their own authenticity. Equally pretending that authentic leadership is just a question of being yourself does a disservice to the complexities and nuances inherent in that aspiration (Taylor, 2013: 186). Authenticity is not a discrete quality that you either possess or you don't – for authenticity to be 'authentic' a quality of detachment and fluidity is needed, otherwise there is a danger of shaping 'reality' to give us an illusion of congruency. Paradoxically then we need to authentically accept our own moments of incoherence and incongruence if we are to truly embark on a journey towards authentic leadership. However, this is not an invitation to get so trapped with our own mental activity that we lose touch with the people we are leading and the context in which we are operating. If we get too tangled in the workings of our mind, our effectiveness as leaders will be reduced as the cognitive energy that will be left to perceive what is around us will be severely diminished. What to do then? As aforementioned, mindfulness may help us to be aware of what is happening within us but also around us (Boyatzis and McKee, 2005). From a mindful state authenticity comes from witnessing our inner communication while being non-judgemental and non-attached to it. This will allow us to be truly open to what is within and without.

At this point you may be wondering, 'why is this level of complexity, accepted confusion and fluidity necessary for authentic leaders? Why would anyone want to dedicate so much intense and invisible inner work to acquire this initially intangible quality?' The work by Otto Scharmer (2009) and Peter Senge and colleagues (2010) emphasises how the internal state of the leader has a profound impact on their external actions and their influence on others. And at the fundamental level, leadership's first commandment is 'know thyself' (Wetlaufer, 2001). Let me share with you an example of the negative implications that result when this commandment is not followed. The CEO of that small company I used as an example above (let's call her Rachel) did not engage in a process of self-awareness. She was, like many CEOs, so busy that she had almost no time for introspection. One year, in my one-to-one meetings with employees I discovered that there was something unusual happening with Rachel. She was behaving in an extremely controlling manner and she was interfering with employees' daily work. Rachel was explicitly showing her employees that she did not trust them and that was very demotivating for them. Through a series of conversations and coaching sessions with Rachel I discovered that the problem lied 'buried' within hidden, unresolved personal issues. To give you a brief picture, employees organised a Christmas night out and did not invite her. For other CEOs this may have been completely acceptable or even encouraged. But for Rachel, this activated an old pain of 'being abandoned', which made her feel extremely hurt by her employees' decision.

In turn, she felt that she could not trust anyone, and at a deeper level she reacted unconsciously from a place of vengeance. Without the appropriate conversations and coaching she would not have realised that the problem was 'hers' and she would have continued controlling her employees and blaming them for the lack of motivation.[1]

I strongly believe that deep inner training which truly puts us in touch with our inner state is key in bringing us closer to our inner and outer realities. This inner training also needs to allow us to witness our attachments (e.g. to our self-image). On this note, what I say to my MBA students and other leaders is the following: if you want to discover who the person underneath your skin is, welcome a journey that will be enriching but may not always be easy and in which you are likely to encounter contradictions within yourself. Enjoy the connection with your thoughts and your emotions, relish the inner gifts that you will discover on your way. If you witness contradictions, simply accept them and do not judge them, just see them from a detached place and be curious. Ask yourself where are these contradictions coming from? In this journey be prepared to find some aspects of yourself which you may not like (some people call them shadows). If you don't find those for a long time, that is OK too.[2]

Question for reflection and discussion

1. How would you describe yourself as a leader? And, how do you think other members of your teams would describe you? Write down as many terms as you can think of that describe your leadership, and then ask others around you to do the same.
2. Think about the face that you present to others with whom you work. Which aspects of yourself do you offer to your colleagues? Which aspects might you not reveal to them?
3. Thinking about your own beliefs, what values are most important to you? How completely or incompletely do you live them when you are leading?
4. When do you find it easy to be at your most authentic? When is it sometimes harder for you to be authentic? What factors may contribute to making authenticity harder to grasp and hold? Write down a list of the latter, and consider what you might do to overcome them.

5. As a leader, when the environment changes around you, what aspects of yourself do you adapt to meet the change? What remains the same? Does your own leadership style itself change over time?

Notes

1 If while you are reading this you catch yourself thinking 'that is because she is a woman' just be aware that these personal issues have nothing to do with gender. Unfortunately, there are many people who have abandonment issues, but they may not be aware of them or they have them so well covered that they cannot find a connection between their reactions and the root cause.

2 It took me three years from the time I first encountered the concept of 'shadows' to discover my first one. My ego created such a perfect self-definition that I couldn't see shadows as they didn't fit with the image I had created for myself. Once I witnessed my mind acting from a shadow it was time for celebration, 'Yes! I've got one'. In time the other shadows are revealing themselves, this is a life-long journey.

Recommended reading

Boyatzis, R. and McKee, A. (2005) *Resonant Leadership: Renewing Yourself and Connecting with Others Through Mindfulness, Hope and Compassion*. Boston, MA: Harvard Business School Press Books.

George, B. (2003) *Authentic Leadership: Rediscovering the Secrets to Creating Lasting Value*. San Francisco, CA: Jossey-Bass.

Goffee, R. and Jones, G. (2005) Managing authenticity: the paradox of great leaders. *Harvard Business Review* 83(12): 86–94.

Haslam, S.A., Reicher, S.D. and Platow M.J. (2011) *The New Psychology of Leadership: Identity, Influence and Power*. East Sussex: Psychology Press.

Ladkin, D. and Taylor, S. (2010) Enacting the 'true self': towards a theory of embodied authentic leadership. *The Leadership Quarterly* 21: 64–74.

Nyberg, D. and Sveningsson, S. (2014) Paradoxes of authentic leadership: leader identity struggles. *Leadership* 10(4): 437–455.

Senge, P., Scharmer, C.O., Jaworski, J. and Flowers, B.S. (2010) *Presence: Exploring Profound Change in People, Organizations and Society*. London: Nicholas Brealey Publishing.

References

Adarves-Yorno, I. (2013) Becoming an authentic leader: reconciling the paradoxes. *EOandP Journal of the Association for Management Education and Development* 20: 73–78 (Special Issue on Leadership Paradoxes).

Avolio, B.J. (2011) *Full Range Leadership Development* (second edition). London: SAGE Publications, Inc.

Avolio, B.J. and Gardner, W.L. (2005) Authentic leadership development: getting to the root of positive forms of leadership. *Leadership Quarterly* 16: 315–338.

Avolio, B.J., Luthans, F. and Walumbwa, F.O. (2004) Authentic leadership: theory-building for veritable sustained performance. Working paper, Gallup Leadership Institute, University of Nebraska-Lincoln.

Avolio, B.J., Gardner, W.L., Walumbwa, F.O., Luthans, F. and May, D.R. (2004) Unlocking the mask: a look at the process by which authentic leaders impact follower attitudes and behaviors. *The Leadership Quarterly* 15: 801–823.

Boyatzis, R. and McKee, A. (2005) *Resonant Leadership: Renewing Yourself and Connecting with Others Through Mindfulness, Hope and Compassion*. Boston, MA: Harvard Business School Press Books.

Endrissat, N., Muller, W.R. and Kaudela-Baum, S. (2007) En route to an empirically-based understanding of authentic leadership. *European Management Journal* 25(3): 207–220.

Epstein, R.M. (1999) Mindful practice. *The Journal of American Medical Association* 282(9): 833–839.

Fields, D. (2013) Essay: followers' assessments of a leader's authenticity: what factors affect how others deem a leader to be authentic? In D. Ladkin and C. Spiller (eds), *Authentic Leadership: Clashes, Convergences and Coalesences* (pp. 133–151). Cheltenham: Edward Elgar.

Gardiner, R. (2013) Cameo: a powerful antidote: Hannah Arendt's concept uniqueness and the discourse of authentic leadership. In D. Ladkin and C. Spiller (eds), *Authentic Leadership: Clashes, Convergences and Coalesences* (pp. 65–68). Cheltenham: Edward Elgar.

Gardner, H. (1995) Reflections on multiple intelligences. *Phi Delta Kappan* 77(3): 200–208.

Gardner, W.L., Cogliser, C.C., Davis, K.M. and Dickens, M.P. (2011) Authentic leadership: a review of the literature and research agenda. *The Leadership Quarterly* 22: 1120–1145.

George, B. and Sims, P. (2007) *True North: Discover Your Authentic Leadership*. San Francisco, CA: Jossey-Bass.

Goffee, R. and Jones, G. (2005) Managing authenticity: the paradox of great leaders. *Harvard Business Review* 83(12): 86–94.

Harter, S. (2002) Authenticity. In C.R. Snyder and S. Lopez (eds), *Handbook of Positive Psychology* (pp. 382–394). Oxford: Oxford University Press.

Haslam, S.A., Reicher S.D. and Platow M.J. (2011) *The New Psychology of Leadership: Identity, Influence and Power*. East Sussex: Psychology Press.

Ibarra, H. (2015) The authenticity paradox: why feeling like a fake can be a sign of growth. *Harvard Business Review* 93: 52–59.

Ilies, R., Morgeson, F.P. and Nahrgang J.D. (2005) Authentic leadership and eudaemonic well-being: understanding leader–follower outcomes. *The Leadership Quarterly* 16: 373–394.

Jeanrenaud, S., Adarves-Yorno, I. and Forsans, N. (2015) Exploring a one planet mindset and its relevance in a transition to a sustainable economy. *Building Sustainable Legacies Journal* 5: 57–79.

Kabat-Zinn, J. (2011) *Wherever You Go, There You Are: Mindfulness Meditation for Everyday Life*. London: Piatkus.

Kernis, M.H. (2003) Toward a conceptualization of optimal self-esteem. *Psychological Inquiry* 14(1): 1–26.

Ladkin, D. and Taylor, S. (2010) Enacting the 'true self': towards a theory of embodied authentic leadership. *The Leadership Quarterly* 21: 64–74.

Lid-Falkman, L. (2014) Appear authentic! The rhetorical oxymoron of authentic leadership. In K.G. Schuyler, J.E. Baugher, K. Jironet and L. Lid-Falkman (eds), *Leading with Spirit, Presence, and Authenticity: A Volume in the International Leadership Association Series, Building Leadership Bridges* (pp. 149–156). San Francisco, CA: Jossey-Bass.

McGonigal, K. (2012) *The Neuroscience of Change: A Compassion-Based Guide to Personal Transformation*. Boulder, CO: Sounds True.

Nyberg, D. and Sveningsson, S. (2014) Paradoxes of authentic leadership: leader identity struggles. *Leadership* 10(4): 437–455.

Roccas, S. and Brewer, M. (2002) Social identity complexity. *Personality and Social Psychology Review* 6(2): 88–106.

Scharmer, C.O. (2009) *Theory U: Leading from the Future as it Emerges*. San Francisco, CA: Berrett-Koehler Publishers.

Senge, P., Scharmer, C.O., Jaworski, J. and Flowers, B.S. (2010) *Presence: Exploring Profound Change in People, Organizations and Society*. London: Nicholas Brealey Publishing.

Shamir, B. and Eilam, G. (2005) 'What's your story?': a life-stories approach to authentic leadership development. *The Leadership Quarterly* 16(3): 395–417.

Tajfel, H. and Turner, J.C. (1979) An integrative theory of intergroup conflict. In W.G. Austin and S. Worchel (eds), *The Social Psychology of Intergroup Relations* (pp. 33–47). Pacific Grove, CA: Brooks/Cole.

Taylor, S.S. (2013) Essay: authentic leadership and the status trap. In D. Ladkin and C. Spiller (eds), *Authentic Leadership: Clashes, Convergences and Coalesences* (pp. 176–187). Cheltenham: Edward Elgar.

Turner, J.C., Hogg, M.A., Oakes, P.J., Reicher, S.D. and Wetherell, M.S. (1987) *Rediscovering the Social Group: A Self-Categorization Theory*. Cambridge, MA: Basil Blackwell.

Wetlaufer, S. (2001) The business against case revolution: an interview with Nestlé's Peter Brabeck. *Harvard Business Review* 79(2): 112–119.

Wilson, V. (2013) Viewpoint: the authentic leader reconsidered: intergrating the marvellous, mundane and mendacious. In D. Ladkin and C. Spiller (eds), *Authentic Leadership: Clashes, Convergences and Coalesences* (pp. 55–64). Cheltenham: Edward Elgar.

8

THE PARADOX OF RIGHT AND WRONG

Jennifer Board

In this chapter, Jennifer Board explores the territory of ethics and leadership and the difficulties that are inherent when values come into conflict with one another. The right course of action may become unclear. We may even face a choice between two apparent wrongs. Jennifer brings a wealth of diverse experience having worked as an army officer, a district commissioner for the girl guides, a primary school teacher, an English tutor, a training officer and numerous Human Resources roles in media, manufacturing, banking and insurance, which together involved her living in Germany, Belize, New York, Singapore, Hong Kong and London.

Right and Wrong, Good and Evil, Virtue and Vice, Innocence and Sin, Justice and Crime, Courage and Cowardice – who defines or decides? If only the world was black and white, decisions would be more straightforward and so much easier to make. However, the world is often experienced as many shades of grey through which we must navigate our life's journey.

When I started out on my career, initially as a junior army officer in 1976, I was sure that I knew the difference between right and wrong, virtue and vice and so on. However, it is our experiences as we move through life that forge us; our achievements, successes and particularly our failures which cause us to question previously strongly held views and enable us to open our minds and truly learn.

Apart from spending five years as an army officer, I held a variety of diverse positions including as a district commissioner for the girl guides, a primary school teacher, an English tutor, a training officer and numerous Human Resources roles in media, manufacturing, banking and insurance. These jobs over thirty-five years involved my living in Soest (Germany), Belize City, New York, Singapore, Hong Kong and London. This experience has proved to be a rich seam from which to mine examples of the best and the worst which human behaviour has to offer. It has certainly seasoned my views on absolute concepts, and demonstrated to me the paradoxes which life, personally and professionally, presents on a regular basis.

From where do our notions of right and wrong emanate? How did we develop a conscience? What is a conscience? The *Oxford English Dictionary* defines conscience as 'a person's moral sense of right and wrong, viewed as acting as a guide to one's behaviour'. However, from where do we gain this moral sense? Is it our upbringing by our parents, our education by our teachers, the pressure exerted by our peers, the beliefs of spiritual leaders, the behaviours of role models we admire? It could be one or a number of these influences in our childhood and adolescence, or another altogether.

In which circumstances do we experience the paradox? Not from the choice between black and white nor between the absolute right and wrong. The paradox is to be found in having to choose between two opposing rights or even the lesser of two wrongs. Examples of this right-versus-right paradox outlined by Kidder (2005: 91), in his book *Moral Courage*, are: truth-telling versus loyalty, of justice versus mercy, of the needs of the individual versus the needs of the community, and short term versus long term. This dilemma is defined by Kidder as: 'when one of our values raises powerful moral arguments for one course of action, while another value raises equally powerful arguments for an opposite course, we find we can't do both. Yet we must act' (2005: 86).

Examples of a wrong-versus-wrong paradox are just as challenging. Is lying always wrong? If not, when is it permissible? Would you lie to avoid hurting someone's feelings? Would you want someone else to lie to avoid hurting your feelings?

These choices are at the centre of the paradox where even a decision not to act is a decision in itself. As pointed out by Margaret

McLean (1996), 'we need to remember that how we decide is just as important as what we decide'.

Ethics

No analysis of right and wrong, or the paradoxes contained therein, would be complete without the foundation stone of ethics. 'The field of ethics (or moral philosophy) involves systematizing, defending and recommending concepts of right and wrong behavior' (Feiser, 2015). Philosophers usually divide ethical theories into three general areas:

1. Meta Ethics – 'the study of the origin and meaning of ethical concepts' particularly '(1) metaphysical issues concerning whether morality exists independent of humans, and (2) psychological issues concerning the underlying mental base of our moral judgments and conduct' (Feiser, 2015).
2. Normative Ethics – 'involves arriving at moral standards that regulate right and wrong conduct'; 'a search for an ideal litmus test of proper behaviour' (Feiser, 2015).
3. Applied Ethics – 'branch of ethics which consists of the analysis of specific, controversial moral issues such as abortion, animal rights or euthanasia'; in recent years, 'subdivided into convenient groups such as medical ethics, business ethics, environmental ethics and sexual ethics' (Feiser, 2015).

Our personal ethics are at the heart of how and what we decide. We may make a quick decision in some circumstances or agonise over the options before us but, if given a free and unfettered choice, we will access our inner core or 'nuclear self' (as identified by Heinz Kohut, 1985: 8, 10) in order to seek alignment between our outward behaviour and inner principles and values. Kohut was a leading American psychoanalyst who defined this core as containing an 'individual's most enduring values' and 'most deeply anchored goals' (1985: 11). When asking what prompts the individual to display moral courage and to 'move forward, despite intimidation from within and without' along 'his lonely road', he found that it was a compulsion to 'shape the pattern of his life . . . in accordance with the design of the nuclear self' (1985: 9). Kidder (2005) agrees with this concept and defines moral courage as 'an alignment of outward acts with inner principles'.

However, what are the foundations of our personal ethics and how we built or acquired them? Within most societies religion, literature and science play an important role in shaping our understanding of the world and for articulating the moral choices and dilemmas that we face. They also, however, contain their own paradoxes, as outlined below.

Religion

Religion has played a significant part for many people in the definition and categorisation of right and wrong.

As far as Christianity and Judaism are concerned, the concepts of right and wrong were defined by God during the Fall of Man from the Garden of Eden. In short, Eve gave Adam fruit from the forbidden tree of the knowledge of good and evil, and in the word of the Bible they were then expelled from Paradise by God 'to till the ground from which he [Adam] was taken'.

The Book of Genesis goes on to further illustrate original sin, crime and punishment through the stories of Cain's banishment to wander the earth after the murder of his brother Abel; of the building of Noah's Ark and the great flood because 'the earth was corrupt . . . and . . . filled with violence'; and the destruction of the 'wicked' cities of Sodom and Gomorrah.

However, it was not until the setting down of the Ten Commandments through Moses that there was a specific biblical definition of the rules or values by which mankind was meant to live, for example, you shall not kill, you shall not commit adultery, you shall not steal, you shall not bear false witness against your neighbour.

Other world religions also specify the right and wrong behaviours expected from their followers. The Eightfold Path of Buddhism specifies a series of interconnected behaviours which define a 'right' way of living – i.e. 'Right View, Right Aspiration, Right Speech, Right Action, Right Livelihood, Right Effort, Right Mindfulness, Right Concentration' (Boeree, 1997). These have a certain degree of overlap with the Ten Commandments of Christianity and Judaism, although they are not a complete match.

Similarly, normative ethics are an important part of the lives of the Hindu people. In the *Bhagavad Gita*, there are 'lists of moral behaviors and a large number of virtues such as purity of mind, non-violence, freedom from anger, renunciation, liberty from covetousness, gentleness, modesty, truth and uprightness' (Biswas, 2014).

The core beliefs and religious practices of Islam state that it is essential that the believer live a good life as defined by the teachings of the Qur'an. An early writer on Muslim philosophy was al-Farabi who appeared 'to have followed Aristotle's lead in dividing the virtues into moral (practical) and intellectual' parts, citing the former as 'temperance, courage, liberality, justice' and the latter as 'practical reasoning, good judgment, sagacity and sound understanding' (Fakhry, 1998).

Although the above five world religions define right and wrong in different ways, they each use their respective definitions as a base against which to judge the behaviours of their followers. Some of the concepts are also relatively similar (indicating a certain commonality of view) as illustrated in the following two examples:

- shall not kill/commit adultery/steal (Christianity, Judaism), right action (Buddhism), non-violence/liberty from covetousness (Hinduism), temperance/justice (Islam);
- bearing false witness (Christianity, Judaism), right speech (Buddhism), truth (Hinduism), justice (Islam).

Despite this apparent commonality, however, there are also a number of obvious paradoxes, such as: why was it seen as a good thing in the Garden of Eden that Adam and Eve remain ignorant? Is the caste system inherent in Hinduism an ethical construct or indeed a mechanism that promotes inequality in society? Where is the temperance and justice in honour killings of Muslim women?

Literature

Literature, likewise, has developed our sense of good and evil through countless poets and authors. The choice of material is so wide that, in the interests of time, I have sketched out below examples from just three of the most well-known poets/authors in classical English literature along with some of the paradoxes inherent in these particular works.

John Milton's best-known work *Paradise Lost* (his interpretation of man's fall from grace and his moral intention to justify the ways of God) is concerned throughout with the causes of evil, the already fallen society of devils and Satan's role in that universe. Milton creates archetypal good characters in the archangels Raphael and Michael who support God, and bad characters in the rebel angels Mammon and Beelzebub who support Satan/Lucifer. The paradox here, of course, is that if God was indeed the creator of all things then he must have created evil as well as good. Why would an omnipotent being do such a thing? Perhaps to give man free choice over how to live his life?

William Shakespeare's plays usually revolve around a tragic hero – Hamlet, Othello, Macbeth, Romeo – who all are undermined by a tragic flaw or a 'tragic virtue', according to James Hammersmith (1990). The strength (good) that made the hero successful initially, and helped him to endure hardship, eventually leads to his undoing through becoming an overdone strength (bad) in the particular circumstances in which he finds himself. Without the hero being worthy of being admired in the first place, his downfall would not be a tragedy. It is the juxtaposition of the opposites of right and wrong, good and bad, success and failure, and the interplay between the two, which makes these plays so compelling. The paradox is how the virtues of the Shakespearean hero lead him and others down the path of disaster.

Charles Dickens' novels present numerous examples of this same type of juxtaposition through placing heroes (good) and villains (bad) in close proximity to each other highlighting the disparity between them, for example, violent Bill Sykes and kind Mr Brownlow in *Oliver Twist*, cruel Daniel Quilp and innocent Little Nell in *The Old Curiosity Shop*. In *David Copperfield* Dickens creates the plot for the optimistic Wilkins Micawber (not a hero) to prove the undoing of the manipulative Uriah Heep (definitely a villain). The paradox here is that it is the feckless, debt-ridden Micawber (who is actually financially reliant on Heep) who, unexpectedly, exposes the fraudulent Heep.

Science

Albert Einstein did not support the view that religion provided the definition of right and wrong. His view was that 'a man's ethical behaviour should be based effectually on sympathy, education, and social ties and needs; no religious basis is necessary. Man would indeed be in a poor way if he had to be restrained by fear of punishment and hopes of reward after death' (einsteinandreligion.com). However, Einstein was not an atheist. He believed in 'Spinoza's God who reveals himself in the orderly harmony of what exists' (godandscience.org). Spinoza in turn was a pantheist who identified God with nature (www.pantheism.net).

There is a scientific theory, espoused by Michael Shermer (a noted historian of science) that attempts to explain why humans know the difference between right and wrong. He calls this a 'scientific theory of morality' (Shermer, 2005). Shermer does not believe that this fundamental knowledge is derived from religious teaching, literature or parental influence but from evolution. In his evolutionary theory, Shermer explains that since humans are 'a hierarchical social primate species . . . as such we need rules and morals and a social structure to enforce them' (2005). He references the science of evolutionary ethics, founded by Charles Darwin, as a subdivision of the larger science of evolutionary psychology, which 'attempts a scientific study of all social and psychological human behaviour' (2005). His view is that human behaviour evolved latterly over hundreds of thousands of years as hunter-gatherers, and this is when the foundations of moral principles were laid down, 'the deepest moral thoughts, behaviours and sentiments belong not just to individuals, or to individual cultures, but to the entire species' (2005).

However, Shermer's theory does not acknowledge that different cultures may attribute different weighting to certain elements. Some examples of the impact of this type of cultural clash of values, such as abortion, adultery, divorce and the rights of women, were explored by Susan Moller Okin (2001) in her article and presentation entitled 'Is Multiculturalism Bad for Women?'

Moral dilemmas and decision-making

The definition of a moral dilemma is one in which the decision about what action to take is not a straightforward one. As already outlined, in some circumstances, a person must choose between right and right when more than one absolute impinges on the situation, therefore being compelled to choose the greater good, or to take no action at all (which is in itself an action). The paradox creates the moral dilemma.

Kidder (2005) outlines a framework incorporating three resolution principles for decision-making when faced with right versus right ethical issues that emerge when two of our core values come into conflict with each other:

- Ends-based principle (also known as utilitarianism) which involves doing 'the greatest good for the greatest number', developed by the English philosophers Jeremy Bentham and John Stuart Mill; focuses on achieving 'good outcomes and results' for the majority rather than on the motives of the decision-maker or any guiding rules.
- Rule-based principle which 'takes no account of the consequences' of decisions, usually associated with the German philosopher, Immanuel Kant; focuses on the motives of the person carrying out the decision; to act in a morally right way the person must act from 'duty'.
- Care-based principle which is 'rooted' in the concept of 'reciprocity'; 'a compassionate standard of great antiquity that lies at the core of all of the world's great religions'; focuses on imagining how the individual would feel if the action being considered was applied to the individual.

In moral dilemmas, ethical decisions come to the forefront and the answer is almost never a clear 'yes' or 'no', 'right' or 'wrong'. Where corporate profits are concerned, the water can become considerably murkier.

One of the top automotive engineering failures in corporate history was that of the Ford Pinto fuel tanks (Gioia, 1992; Wojdyla, 2011). In this example, Ford's management made the decision that it would cost less to pay damages to customers who were injured by the car's fuel tank catching fire than it would cost to add tank shields to prevent punctures – an additional cost of approximately US$11 per vehicle. Quite apart from the questionable ethics of this decision, it actually cost Ford far more in the end, in part because of the damages awarded to injured individuals and bereaved families, but particularly because of the public relations disaster which negatively impacted the credibility of the company and the brand. For many years, Ford retained the toxic reputation of putting profits before safety, which lost it many customers.

We, all of us, use some individual process or priorities to make ethical decisions. Whether we consider the impact of the results, follow the rules we learned in childhood, the behaviour of role models or some other mechanism, we each have some foundation on which we base our judgements.

Interactive exercise

Let us now pause and consider our own ethical decision-making.

> *Think of a recent ethical/moral dilemma that you have experienced either at work or at home.*
>
> *Consider this memory for five minutes, remembering what the options were, why you made the decision you did, what rationale you used and what (if any) were the consequences then and for your future decision-making.*
>
> *If you are studying this chapter as part of a group, split into pairs for ten minutes and discuss these individual moral dilemmas.*
>
> *What have you learned from this exercise?*
>
> *Perhaps you have become aware of the base you draw upon when conflicted and faced with a challenging decision in either your personal or professional life?*

Relevance to leadership

Uncovering the values that drive us is all very well but what is its significance to our leadership?

Two leadership theories particularly (although neither are perfect models) support the viewpoint that this awareness is fundamental to the understanding and exercise of effective leadership. One is authentic leadership, as outlined by George and Sims (2007) in *True North*. In this book, the authors devote considerable space to encouraging the reader to discover their 'authentic self' and through that insight to discovering their authentic leadership. They believe this is best done by testing ourselves, our values and our beliefs through real-world experiences. George and Sims believe that before an individual can test any of this, they first need to 'understand (their) values' principles and motivations 'and then determine (their) leadership principles'.

The authors believe that our values are derived from our beliefs and convictions – deciding what is most important in our lives. There is no one set of right values, instead we all have to decide for ourselves what is right or wrong for us. This is also the moral relativist's view, claiming 'that what is right for one person is not necessarily right for another' (Horner, 2014). Indeed, different values may be more important to individuals at different times of their lives, for example, building a career versus building a family.

Our leadership principles are our values translated into action, which lead us to establish our individual ethical boundaries. These are essential issues to establish which usually emerge through time, experience and interaction with others. These boundaries are important to our effectiveness and wellbeing, as it is when we are under pressure – tired, stressed, conflicted – that we most need a firm foundation on which to depend. As George and Sims (2007) ask, 'do you know what your life and your leadership are all about, and when you are being true to yourself?'

Authentic leadership theory has its limitations and detractors (see also Chapter 7 in this book). In their paper critiquing the notion of authentic leadership, Ford and Harding (2011) suggest that 'authentic leadership as an indication of a leader's true self is impossible and . . . attempts at its implementation could lead to destructive dynamics within organizations'. Personally, whilst I am sympathetic to the criticism that this theory does not allow the leader to reveal negative characteristics (i.e. a dark side), the compelling part of this theory is surely the encouragement of leaders to demonstrate the moral courage to tap into their core beliefs and to behave professionally in alignment with these. This action will, itself, cause individuals to examine whether or not their chosen profession or current organisation reflect these inner values. Ford and Harding's suggestion that the authentic leader's role 'is to ensure followers are themselves no more than objects . . . reshaped and subsumed into the service of . . . the leader and the organization's values' (2011: 475) rather overstates the case, forgetting that the driving force behind authentic leadership theory is to encourage leaders to discover what their 'life and leadership are all about', not to encourage the 'domination/suppression' of their followers.

Another leadership theory which is supportive of the importance of a leader's beliefs and self-awareness is James Scouller's three levels of leadership model (Scouller, 2011: 56) which specifies the three levels as Public, Private and Personal. This model is usually illustrated as three concentric circles and four arrows pointing outwards from the central core of personal leadership. The outer two levels are behavioural and the third level is the inner person.

According to Scouller, the two outer circles – Public and Private Leadership – contain thirty-four distinct public leadership behaviours and a further fourteen private leadership behaviours. Based on my professional experience of defining, developing and implementing leadership competencies and behaviours over many years, such a large number of leadership behaviours, practically speaking, would appear to be extremely time-consuming to implement in a commercial enterprise. However, the inner Personal Leadership circle appears more compelling as it concerns a person's leadership presence, knowhow, skills, beliefs, emotions and unconscious habits. For beliefs, emotions and unconscious habits, we could interpret values, ethics, the power which drives us and the bedrock against which a leader can make the difficult decisions necessary in any leadership journey.

As Scouller says, 'at its heart is the leader's self-awareness, his progress toward self-mastery and technical competence, and his sense of connection with those around him. It's the inner core, the source, of a leader's outer leadership effectiveness' (2011). This is a powerful argument for the importance of that inner core, that nuclear self which governs the actions of an effective leader.

Organisational and personal values

Culture and values are driven by the leadership of the business – the two are indivisible. If leaders are not effective role models for the type of behaviour they want to encourage, no one will believe what they say; they will watch what they do and take their lead from there.

Unfortunately, the development of these values is misunderstood by some business leaders who decide themselves what the business's values will be and then tell the employees what theirs should be. Little wonder that, in these companies, there is often negligible buy-in from the employee population. The imposed values are then, of course, published on the company's website, and/or printed on T-shirts and coffee mugs where they are routinely ignored, including by the CEO/business leader who put them there in the first place. This is just another example of something which looks good in the annual report or company website but often has no real meaning or traction within an organisation unless there is a corresponding focus on the issue, for example, 'people are our greatest asset' seems impressive as a corporate statement but only if there is corresponding action which demonstrates its importance.

There is no need for corporate values to be emblazoned on T-shirts or coffee mugs if they are embedded into all the facets, the very fabric, of an organisation and demonstrably lived. As the well-known mantra goes, 'watch my feet, not my lips' (McNealy, 1996).

Impact of ethical leadership

The impact of effective and ineffective leadership should not be underestimated. This does not just mean competence to lead but also the ethics demonstrated by the leader.

Unethical leadership can destroy a company and its reputation very quickly as witnessed through the imploding of BCCI, Enron, WorldCom, Long-Term Capital Management (LTCM), the *News of the World*, to name but a few.

It is interesting to consider why and when all these organisations began the slide from hero to zero. Was it fear of failure and bankruptcy which prompted the senior executives of Enron and WorldCom to manipulate accounting rules? (Mohr, 2013). Unfortunately, the collapse of Enron also led to the collapse of its auditor Arthur Andersen, which was once seen as the gold standard of accounting (Folger, 2011). Was it when the ends seemed to justify the means that *News of the World* journalists began hacking telephones? Although not all their journalists indulged in this practice, the tarnish stuck to the brand and by association to the employees themselves.

International dimension

It is even more important these days in this increasingly connected global business world to consider the cultural differences that may exist in definitions of right and wrong. Although both the US and UK governments have attempted to level the playing field globally with anti-corruption legislation in the form of legislation such as the US Foreign Corrupt Practices Act 1977 (amended 1998) and the UK Bribery Act 2010 there are still practices which exist in some regions which, those who operate them, find practical and necessary. An example is facilitation payments (Kelly, 2013), which are a common way in a number of countries of ensuring a telephone is fitted, an electricity supply is connected or a container of household belongings are released from the docks.

Similarly, when attending a business meeting in some overcrowded cities in developing countries, a business executive may sit for hours in traffic if the local police chief has not been commissioned to provide motorbike outriders to escort the car to the office.

Although these practices may not seem reasonable or appropriate to a Western audience, nevertheless they exist for practical reasons. Of course, sometimes things go wrong, particularly with alleged facilitation payments as we know from several high profile cases involving global companies, such as BAE in Saudi Arabia, BP in Russia or GSK in China. The investigations into the business ethics of, and bribery allegations made against, FIFA are another case in point, with new insights continuing to emerge.

The key point here is to be aware that operating in other regions in the world is not the same as in the US or UK. We may all be more connected now but different norms may apply. The challenge here is in deciding when this practice is within acceptable business norms and when it is a practice that needs to be challenged. This challenge to an accepted status quo, and potentially the vested interests of powerful individuals and groups, is likely to require the demonstration of a considerable degree of moral courage. Indeed a challenge not for the faint-hearted.

Moral courage

The first time I thought about moral courage as a leadership capability, I was attending the Leadership conference of a large financial institution, listening to a particularly engaging presentation by the late Rush Kidder. Listening to Rush, it became clear to me that this topic would be most interesting to research in order to make sense of some of the behaviour I had witnessed during my career, for example, people making the expedient choice at the expense of the ethical choice; the political decision at the expense of the brave decision; and giving the disingenuous answer at the expense of the truth.

One of the models in his book *Moral Courage* (Kidder, 2005: 73) illustrates his definition of the three elements of moral courage. Kidder describes these elements as: a commitment to moral *Principles*, an awareness of the *Danger* involved in supporting these principles, and a willing *Endurance* of that danger. At the centre of these intersecting domains is moral courage. Kidder also believed that moral courage could be taught, encouraged and developed in individuals and organisations (Kidder, 2005). He believed this could be learned by:

- Discourse and Discussion – where the language of rational enquiry clarifies the idea of moral courage and renders it explicable and relevant;
- Modeling and Mentoring – where real-life exemplars demonstrate moral courage in action and chart pathways of human endeavor that others can follow;
- Practice and Persistence – where learners can discipline themselves through direct, incremental skill building that increases their ability to apply moral courage.

Kidder is not the only person who thought moral courage could be taught. Both Plato and Aristotle believed that education was central to moral development: 'the education of our emotional responses is crucial for the development of virtuous character. If our emotional responses are educated properly, we will learn to take pleasure or pain in the right things' (Homiak, 2015).

Kidder provides us with his moral courage checklist, showing how to avoid inhibitors to courage including the following: overconfident cultures, compromises, timidity, tepid ethics, bystander apathy, groupthink and cultural differences. Having experienced some of these inhibitors in organisations, I can relate professionally to elements of this checklist. In an organisation where moral courage is not encouraged, people feel unable to confront reality and say what they really think. This type of climate is not conducive to supporting the constructive feedback necessary to inform leaders about what is happening in their organisation. If this open approach were in existence, there would be less need for whistleblowing. According to Lilanthi Ravishankar (2003), 'to prevent whistleblowing, encourage whistleblowing'.

Whistleblowers

Are whistleblowers morally courageous, or could they just be troublemakers? (Ravishankar, 2013). It very much depends on their motives.

Immanuel Kant's rule-based principle for resolving moral dilemmas emphasises the importance of motives. Some whistleblowers have good cause to alert the public to dangers, both physical and moral, and through this they serve the good of society. However, how is it possible to know if their whistleblowing is authentic and not just the action of a disenchanted employee seeking revenge?

The willingness to confront a situation for the sake of what is right, independent of the cost, is not an easy thing to do. In her article 'Moral Courage in the Workplace', Catherine Capozzi (2013) points out the benefits of improving or transforming corporate culture, creating a more equitable workplace and helping better society. However, she also points out that showing this type of moral courage may cause isolation from colleagues and attract unwanted attention from the company who may try to discredit the reputation of the whistleblower. Some CEOs may feel that displaying moral courage may tarnish the reputation of their company by exposing wrongdoing, weaken their position as the leader or get in the way of generating profits. Thus, displaying moral courage in the workplace may come at a high cost – both professional and personal. Potentially, this is a lonely road to travel.

However, brave and ethical whistleblowers may take heart from a quote of Winston Churchill: 'You have enemies? Good. That means you've stood up for something, some time in your life' (Petrie, 2013).

Churchill himself is a great example of a leader who was absorbed from his early years with a moral vision for his life (Hayward, 1998). He braved great unpopularity in the years before the Second World War, as he was one of the few political leaders who refused to appease

Adolf Hitler. Historian John Keegan later commented that 'it is the moral rather than the intellectual content of his judgment that dominates' (Blake and Louis, 1993: 327).

Leadership, therefore, requires a certain amount of intellect, but character is key. Mihaly Csikszentmihalyi (2008) writes of people admired for their courage, and includes the example of Ignaz Semmelweis, the Hungarian physician who braved mockery by insisting that the lives of mothers could be saved if obstetricians washed their hands between examining patients. Csikszentmihalyi's view of this type of courage is that 'of all the virtues we can learn no trait is more useful, more essential for survival, and more likely to improve the quality of life' (Csikszentmihalyi, 2008: 200).

Kidder (2005) wrote that although moral courage is an essential characteristic of leadership, paradoxically, it is something that should rarely be necessary to deploy. In his view, if there is a call for this strength to be frequently utilised, then this would be a sign of an unhealthy culture.

Another paradox seen through the lens of a practitioner is that sometimes an individual may need to be pragmatic in order to change an organisation from the inside, i.e. the need is first to survive, and then succeed by not challenging some acts which appear unethical. However, this is a risky strategy, as the siren call from the dark side, with the promise of an easier corporate and professional life, can be compelling and attractive. Once lured by the dark side, regaining the moral high ground may prove difficult. There is a warning here for travellers.

Interactive exercise

Let us now consider our personal views on moral courage.

In the end, is the espousal of moral courage a lost cause?

Is it just too hard to implement no matter how much we may want to model this behaviour?

Is the personal cost too high?

Is it a virtue that can only be deployed by those who have few financial responsibilities, i.e. with nothing to lose?

Are there insufficient role models to inspire us?

Consider these questions for ten minutes and prepare to defend your view.

If you are studying in a group, split into pairs and spend a further ten minutes presenting your argument to each other.

The challenge of the paradox

There are certainly many perplexing questions that arise when considering the definition and categorisation of right and wrong. The answers are likely to depend on personal ethics, which may well be different for various individuals and diverse cultures.

Following the sea change of the 2008 banking crisis, it seems that more and more people are prepared to criticise behaviour which is perceived as immoral, even if it is legal. Examples of this perceived immoral but legal practice include large corporates which avoid paying corporation tax through complex offshore legal structures, excessive bonuses for CEOs whose companies do not perform as promised, expensive termination payments for executives without clear justification, retailers using cheap overseas locations to make clothing for the UK market without ensuring adequate working conditions for the foreign workers who are not covered by UK Health and Safety legislation.

In the past, people mostly would only have concerned themselves if this type of behaviour was illegal. These days, companies have to consider their reputational risk far more than before, as the taxpayer, shareholder and consumer may regard their behaviour as unethical and wield the power of veto, which they always had but seldom used.

The fact that the world is grey, not black and white, provides a challenge and an opportunity for learning which would not be available in a climate of certainty. Having the ability and capacity to embrace and learn from life's inherent paradoxes is an important skill to develop as a leader. It is key to be able to admit when something went wrong so we can learn from the experience, otherwise, we are doomed to repeat our failures.

However, in navigating our path through this complicated life, a moral compass is just as valuable as a physical version to avoid becoming lost. In using a moral compass, what seems most important is that first an individual needs to know his or her own values, otherwise it is not possible to defend them. This 'internal compass' outlined by George and Sims (2007) is similar to the 'nuclear self' referred to by Kohut (1985), a force which is a key driver in our lives.

Building self-awareness is an important step in the journey of personal development. Nevertheless, becoming self-aware is only part of the challenge. Practising our values is the same as exercising a muscle. The more we exercise it, the stronger it gets.

Although, we each may define right and wrong differently, the heart of the matter is that we need to be open-minded enough to accept that, on occasions, the two concepts become blurred and present an altogether more complicated puzzle to solve compared to one based on polarised definitions. Life and leadership are by no means straightforward which is what makes the challenges they present so interesting and, ultimately, so beneficial to both personal and professional development. Indeed, the more leaders learn to work productively with uncertainty and ambiguity, the more adaptable and resilient they should become. However, the need to embrace and learn from life's paradoxes is not only essential to ensure the survival and success of individual business leaders but also that of work teams, organisations and society itself.

Questions for reflection and discussion

1. What examples of behaviours that you regard as 'right' come easily to mind? What examples of 'wrong'? Make a list of each, and consider why you put each example on the list. What makes it 'right' or 'wrong'?
2. Thinking about truth, when would you lie – for example, to avoid hurting someone's feelings? When would you want someone else to lie to you – for example, to avoid hurting your feelings?
3. Think of a recent ethical/moral dilemma that you have experienced either at work or at home. Consider this memory for five minutes, remembering what the options were, why you made the decision you did, what rationale you used and what (if any) were the consequences then and for your future decision-making. If you are studying this chapter as part of a group, you could split into pairs for ten minutes and discuss these individual moral dilemmas. What have you learned from this exercise?

4. What does the organisation you work with most believe in? What are its values? Make a list of these. Then, write down a similar list of your own values and beliefs. How far do the two lists correlate?
5. Even though we consider moral courage to be desirable, might there be times when the personal cost of courage is too high? Under what circumstances would you feel compelled to compromise your principles? Think about this, and discuss the question with others around you to see if they feel the same.

Recommended reading

Capozzi, Catherine (2013) Moral Courage in the Workplace. *Houston Chronicle*, accessed on 27 November 2013 through http://smallbusiness.chron.com/moral-courage-workplace-20589.html.

Csikszentmihalyi, Mihaly (2008) *Flow: The Psychology of Optimal Experience*, New York, NY: Harper & Row.

George, Bill and Sims, Peter (2007) *True North*, San Francisco: Jossey-Bass.

Gioia, D.A. (1992) Pinto Fires and Personal Ethics: A Script Analysis of Missed Opportunities. *Journal of Business Ethics*, 11, 379–389.

Kidder, Rushworth (2005) *Moral Courage*, New York, NY: Harper.

Scouller, James (2011) *The Three Levels of Leadership*, London: Management Books 2000 Limited.

References

Biswas, Paul S. (2014) Ethics of Hinduism in the Light of Christianity, accessed on 16 August 2014 through www.safene.com/hinduethics.htm.

Blake, Robert and Louis, William Roger (1993) *Churchill: A Major New Assessment of His Life in Peace and War*, New York, NY: W.W. Norton & Company.

Boeree, C. George (1997) Towards a Buddhist Psychotherapy, accessed on 26 June 2015 through http://webspace.ship.edu/cgboer/buddhapsych.htm.

Capozzi, Catherine (2013) Moral Courage in the Workplace. *Houston Chronicle*, accessed on 27 November 2013 through http://smallbusiness.chron.com/moral-courage-workplace-20589.html.

Csikszentmihalyi, Mihaly (2008) *Flow: The Psychology of Optimal Experience*, New York, NY: Harper & Row.

Fakhry, Majid (1998) Ethics in Islamic Philosophy, in E. Craig (ed.) *Routledge Encyclopedia of Philosophy*, London: Routledge, pp. 438–442.

Feiser, James (2015) Ethics, *The Internet Encyclopedia of Philosophy* (IEP) ISSN 2161-0002, accessed on 26 June 2015 through www.iep.utm.edu/ethics.

Folger, Jean (2011) *The Enron Collapse: A Look Back*, accessed on 23 October 2014 through http://www.investopedia.com.

Ford, Jackie and Harding, Nancy (2011) The Impossibility of the 'True Self' of Authentic Leadership, *Leadership*, 7(4), 463–479.

George, Bill and Sims, Peter (2007) *True North*, San Francisco: Jossey-Bass.

Gioia, D.A. (1992) Pinto Fires and Personal Ethics: A Script Analysis of Missed Opportunities, *Journal of Business Ethics*, 11, 379–389.

Hammersmith, James (1990) Shakespeare and the Tragic Virtue, *Southern Humanities Review*, 24(3), 245–254, accessed on 16 August 2014 through www.jsu.edu/depart/english/gates/shtragcv.htm.

Hayward, Steven F. (1998) *Churchill on Leadership*, London: Forum.

Homiak, Marcia (2015) Moral Character, *The Stanford Encyclopedia of Philosophy* (Spring 2015 Edition), Edward N. Zalta (ed.), accessed on 28 June 2015 through http://plato.stanford.edu/archives/spr2015/entries/moral-character/.

Horner, Michael (2014) Spirituality: Is There Any Real Right and Wrong?, accessed on 12 August 2014 through www.powertochange.com/discover/faith/questionsaboutgod6/.

Kelly, Matt (2013) Reality of Facilitation Payments, accessed on 16 August 2014 through www.complianceweek.com/blogs/the-big-picture/reality-of-facilitation-payments.

Kidder, Rushworth (2005) *Moral Courage*, New York, NY: Harper.

Kohut, Heinz (1985) *Self Psychology and the Humanities: Reflections on a New Psychoanalytic Approach*, New York, NY: Norton.

McLean, Margaret R. (1996) Making Decisions About Right and Wrong, accessed on 12 August 2014 through www.scu.edu/ethics/practicing/decision/right-wrong.html.

McNealy, R.M. (1996) *Making Quality Happen: A Step By Step Guide to Winning the Quality Revolution*, New York, NY: Chapman and Hall.

Mohr, Angie (2013) 5 Most Publicized Ethics Violations by CEOs, accessed on 23 October 2014 through www.investopedia.com/financial-edge/0113/5-most-publicized-ethics-violations.

Okin, Susan Moller (2001) When Cultural Values Clash with Universal Rights: Is Multiculturalism Bad for Women?, accessed on 12 August 2014 through www.scu.edu/ethics/publications/submitted/okin/multicultural.html.

Petrie, John (2013) John Petrie's Collection of Winston Churchill Quotes, accessed on 8 August 2013 through http://jpetrie.myweb.uga.edu/bulldog.html.

Ravishankar, Lilanthi (2003) Encouraging Internal Whistleblowing in Organizations, accessed on 12 August 2014 through www.scu.edu/ethics/publications/submitted/whistleblowing.html.

Scouller, James (2011) *The Three Levels of Leadership*, London: Management Books 2000 Limited.

Shermer, Michael (2005) *The Science of Good and Evil: Why People Cheat, Gossip, Care, Share, and Follow the Golden Rule*, New York, NY: Times Books/Henry Holt and Company.

Wojdyla, Ben (2011) The Top Automotive Engineering Failures: The Ford Pinto Fuel Tanks, accessed on 22 October 2014 through www.popularmechanics.com/cars/news/industry/top-automotive-engineering-failures.

9

CONCLUSION

Richard Bolden, Morgen Witzel and Nigel Linacre

In this chapter Richard Bolden, Morgen Witzel and Nigel Linacre review some of the key themes emerging in this book and their implications for the ways in which we think about and practice leadership and leadership development. Concepts including negative capability, the social construction of leadership, wicked problems, complexity and boundary spanning leadership are considered in order to illustrate the potential benefits and opportunities of a paradoxical approach to leadership.

> How wonderful that we have met with a paradox. Now we have some hope of making progress.
>
> *(Niels Bohr, physicist)*

This book has explored some of the many paradoxes of leadership theory, practice and development. The rationalist view of organisations, promoted in most popular business literature, tends to struggle with the notion of paradox – suggesting that leadership and management practice should be underpinned by rigorous, evidence-based principles and best practice. Whilst recognising the contribution that this work has made to organisational effectiveness and efficiency, in this book we have argued that such logic – suggesting a relatively simple causal relationship between management and/or leadership practice and organisational outcomes – can be misleading and we have called for deeper engagement with the complexities and uncertainties of organisational life.

The notion of paradox is, of course, not new and nor is its application to the field of leadership and management. The quote from Lao Tzu, cited in Chapters 2 and 3, comes from what is widely regarded as one of the first books ever written on leadership. More recently, in his best-selling book *The Age of Paradox*, Charles Handy suggested:

> We need a new way of thinking about our problems and our futures. My suggestion is the management of paradox, an idea which is itself a paradox, in that paradox can only be 'managed' in the sense of coping with. Management always did mean 'coping with,' until we purloined the word to mean planning and control.
>
> *(Handy, 1994, p. 12)*

Handy will have known, of course, that the term 'manage' derives from the Italian word *maneggiare*, which literally means to put a horse through its paces, and that riding a horse is an act of partnership (of strength and intellect) where neither the rider nor the horse are 'in control'. Handy identified nine enduring paradoxes associated with economic progress, suggesting that whilst they cannot be resolved they can be 'managed'. By way of conclusion he proposed that leaders and managers have a key role to play in helping people to cope with uncertainty through offering 'a sense of continuity, a sense of connection, and a sense of direction' (1994, p. 247) in order to help people navigate their way forward in turbulent times.

Little could Handy have anticipated the actual rate of change over the last two decades, fuelled largely by technological developments that have rendered low-cost, high-power computing and communication accessible to the masses and have totally transformed both business and social interactions.[1] His call for the development of a sense of continuity, connection and direction resonates with work on the role of leadership as sense-making (Smirchich and Morgan, 1982; Pye, 2005; Weick, 2012) but stops short of recent work that attempts to decentre the study of leadership away from the 'tripod' of leader, followers and shared task (Bennis, 2007) to leadership processes and outputs such as direction, alignment and commitment (Drath *et al.*, 2008).

In writing this concluding chapter it would be tempting to propose an integrative framework of leadership paradoxes and to propose a sequence of steps for addressing them. This would, however, be a mistake as in attempting to rationalise paradox we fall back into the usual trap of mainstream management and leadership literature. The power of paradox lies in its ability to push us beyond dualisms (characterised by either/or thinking) to dualities and dialectics (characterised by both/and thinking). Paradox demands us to embrace uncertainty and ambiguity and to hold multiple possibilities in our minds at the same time.

A capacity for pluralistic thought is widely sought after but rare to attain. The British poet John Keats called it 'negative capability' and identified it as a quality that marked out creative genius, as detailed in a letter to his brothers George and Tom in which he reflected on the literary achievements of William Shakespeare:

> several things dove-tailed in my mind, and at once it struck me what quality went to form a Man of Achievement, especially in Literature, and which Shakespeare possessed so enormously – I mean Negative Capability, that is, *when a man is capable of being in uncertainties, mysteries, doubts, without any irritable reaching after fact and reason.*
>
> *(Keats, 1817, cited in Gittings, 1968, p. 43, italics in original)*

More recently the concept of negative capability has been picked up in organisation studies literature and has been proposed as a counterpoint to the typical competencies and qualities demanded of leaders and managers. Simpson *et al.* (2002, p. 1209) suggested that:

> negative capability can create an intermediate space that enables one to continue to think in difficult situations. Where positive capability supports 'decisive action', negative capability supports 'reflective inaction', that is, the ability to resist dispersing into defensive routines when leading at the limits of one's knowledge, resources and trust.

All around the world, however, academics, consultants and HRM professionals continue to advocate and implement organisational practices and developmental processes that emphasise the need for clarity and decisiveness in leadership and management. Whilst a rhetoric of inclusive and shared leadership is gaining traction in many areas, the realities of organisational life appear to have changed little – at least in terms of how recognition and reward tends to go to those in positions of power and influence with little consideration of how others may be systematically excluded or disadvantaged (see, for example, Fletcher, 2002).

Recent events such as the Global Financial Crisis, Occupy Movement, Arab Spring and rise of the Islamic State (ISIS) demonstrate the huge inadequacies of individual and hierarchical models of leadership and the potential for entrenched ways of thinking to render us blind to things that, in retrospect, had been a long time coming. Global management and leadership education, largely driven by US scholarship and practice, however, continues to roll-out a Cartesian-based logic that leaves many fundamental assumptions unchallenged and important questions unasked (Mabey and Mayrhofer, 2015). In the search for 'evidence' and 'answers' we may lose sight of the wood for the trees or mistake the map for the terrain[2] (Bolden and Gosling, 2006, Bolden *et al.*, 2006).

Within this book we have taken a rather different approach – to encourage reflection, debate and critical engagement in order to facilitate alternative ways of seeing and understanding the world. In our quest for better leadership it is all too easy to lose sight of the fact that the journey is often what matters most, that we must each make our own journey and, in many cases, that there may be no ultimate destination (Ciulla, 2006).

The elusive nature of leadership

Whilst reading this book you may have noticed that, although we do define the concept of paradox, no attempt is made to give a clear and consistent definition of leadership. Leadership is an 'essentially contested concept' (Grint, 2005a), where understandings and practices are socially constructed and tend to have more to do with the motivations, beliefs and values of those providing the definition than the evidence on which they are based. As Graeme Salaman summarises in his critique of the leadership and management competency movement:

> The nature of management and managers and of leaders and leadership is highly problematic: there is no agreed view on what managers or leaders should do and what they need to do it. And there never can be, since such definitions arise not from organisational or technical requirements, but from the shifting ways in which over time these functions are variously conceptualised. The manager, as much as the worker, is a product of history.
>
> *(Salaman, 2004, p. 58)*

We are not suggesting, of course, that leadership is non-existent or irrelevant but that it is socially constructed and that any attempt to capture its definitive 'essence' is misguided and likely to result in unintended consequences. As the river metaphor used in Chapter 6 demonstrates – the nature and experience of one's encounters with leadership will be shaped by a wide range of factors and is unlikely to ever be exactly the same again for any individual, let alone others who will experience it from a different perspective.

Instead, we suggest a more fluid engagement with leadership definitions and approaches depending on what one is seeking to achieve and the context in which this is being done. As Joanne Ciulla suggests:

> the scholars who worry about constructing the ultimate definition of leadership are asking the wrong question, but inadvertently trying to answer the right one . . . The ultimate question about leadership is not 'What is the definition of leadership?' The whole point of studying leadership is, 'What is good leadership?' The use of the word *good* here has two senses, morally good and technically good or effective.
>
> *(Ciulla, 2002, pp. 340–341, original emphasis)*

In attempting to develop leaders and leadership for an uncertain and unknowable world we encourage you to look beyond the usual examples espoused in Business School texts to engage with the underlying philosophical assumptions that shape both leadership and organisational practice and life in general. From such a perspective useful leadership learning can emerge from many sources, including politics, history, literature, personal experience, family life and travel (as illustrated throughout this book). The theories and concepts that are introduced within this book should be held lightly. They are offered as frameworks and ideas to support critical thinking and reflection about leadership but any one of them is likely to lead to dysfunctional outcomes if applied with insufficient consideration to their effects within a given context.

In thinking about leadership education, we agree with Amanda Sinclair's (2007) suggestion that it should be founded on the pillars of 'thinking critically', 'working experientially' and 'reflective practice'.

> Leadership is a process of critical and compassionate engagement with the world [. . . It] is a commitment to challenging accepted wisdom, to reflecting deeply on our motives so as to avoid co-option, to being mindful of relations between our bodies and psyches, to being in the moment, and to leading with the intent of freeing – both the self and others.
>
> *(2007, p. xxiv)*

Changing perspectives on leadership and the nature of problems

Whilst the relationship between paradox and leadership is not new and, indeed, has been spoken about many times before, we believe that this book is timely given the growing interest in genuine alternatives to the rhetoric of heroic leadership that has dominated the theory, practice and development of leadership for many years. More recent academic literature on 'post-heroic' leadership has fuelled a surge of interest in the relational, emotional, ethical and embodied aspects of leadership yet until relatively recently has had little direct impact on practice within organisations. There is, however, growing evidence that the situation is beginning to change and concepts such as distributed, shared and collective leadership are now widely used in fields such as education, health and public services (Bolden, 2011).

The argument for more inclusive, shared and emergent leadership is often framed in normative terms – suggesting that it is more ethical or democratic – but is increasingly being supported by evidence that demonstrates the limitations of traditional approaches in the face of the 'wicked' issues that require collaboration and partnership across organisational boundaries.

The distinction between tame and wicked problems, developed by Rittel and Weber (1973), has been popularised in relation to leadership through the work of Professor Keith Grint (2005b, 2008). A 'tame' problem is something that we've either seen before or can apply a specific logic to resolve. Grint suggests that the response to such problems is largely a case of organising a process to address the issue – effectively calling for 'management'. A 'wicked' problem on the other hand is complex and intractable, with no obvious solution. Such a situation, Grint suggests, calls for 'leadership' and is largely about asking questions and mobilising collective expertise to determine the real nature of the problem and weighing up the options. Such problems may appear 'messy' and solutions are often 'clumsy' as people navigate their way through a complex, ambiguous and changing landscape (Grint, 2008).

In addition to tame and wicked problems, Grint identified a third type of problem: 'critical'. A critical problem is defined as urgent, requiring immediate and decisive intervention. In the face of a critical problem leaders and managers need to act fast and may not have time for wider consultation. Such responses may well be autocratic or directive, demanding an answer, whether or not it is necessarily the most inclusive, informed or effective.

A key feature of Grint's framework is that problems are not 'critical', 'tame' or 'wicked' in themselves, but are framed as such through a process of 'social construction'. An illustration of this can be seen in the differing approaches of George W. Bush and John Kerry in the 2004 US presidential election. A decisive feature of this campaign was how the two candidates presented their approach to responding to the threat to US national security posed by the September 11th attacks of 2001 and the subsequent 'War on Terror'. Bush presented this as a 'critical' problem and himself as the commander-in-chief whilst Kerry suggested that it was a 'wicked' problem requiring a shared understanding of the underlying issues and collective debate on potential ways forward. Both candidates engaged in attempts to create a compelling narrative that voters would engage with and follow through when casting their votes. The outcome of the election was incredibly close – 50.7 per cent to 48.3 per cent – yet the position of the two candidates was in stark contrast to one another. Leadership requires followership and, even in a democratic society, the winner frequently takes all.

This example draws attention not only to the varying nature of problems but also to the role of storytelling and narrative in leadership. For leaders to be successful they need to be able to tell a convincing tale and, in a world of 24/7 media, influence others to tell stories on their behalf too. The success or failure of an idea lies not just in its accuracy or utility, but in how it is communicated and interpreted.

Leading in complex systems

Heifetz *et al.* (2009) make a similar distinction to that between tame and wicked problems in their account of adaptive leadership – suggesting that leaders and organisations need to master the ability to shift their perspective from the 'dance floor' to the 'balcony' in order to recognise the wider system in which they are operating. Problems that may appear 'technical' (or tame) up close may well be recognised as 'adaptive' (or 'wicked') from further away, as we recognise the interdependencies and interconnections between different parts of the system.

Take a look at Figure 9.1. You may struggle to recognise that the three pictures are each increasingly 'zoomed-out' views of the same picture. Whilst each is based on the same overall image it is difficult to see exactly how they relate to each other – the first seems relatively simple and ordered, the second is complicated and the third is complex.[3]

However skilful we may be at 'getting on the balcony', though, ours is always a view from somewhere as we can never fully step outside of the systems that we are part of. A common way of trying to work with paradox is to identify the opposing polarities that need to be balanced, for example, cost versus quality, speed versus accuracy, short-term perspective versus long-term perspective. To consider the latter for just a moment, a steady stream of commentators over the past decade have called for business leaders to abandon short-termism

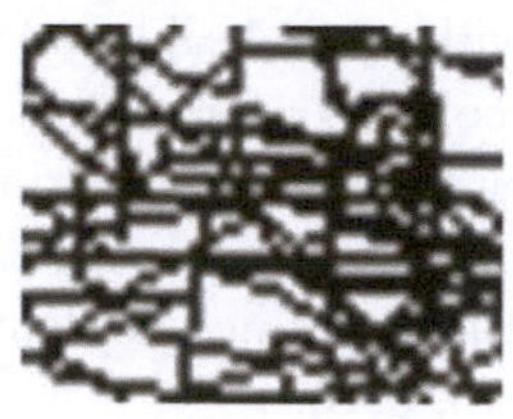
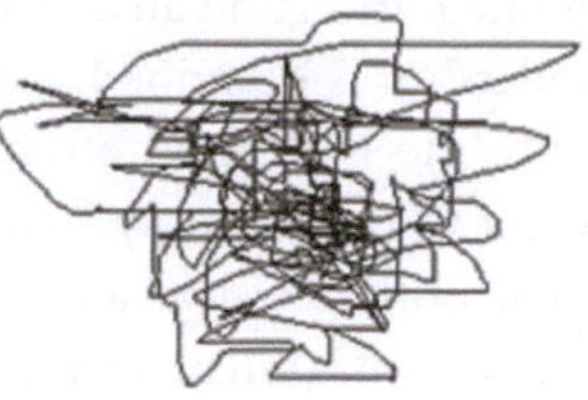

FIGURE 9.1 Three perspectives on a system.

and take a more long-term strategic perspective (see for example Barton, 2011). But can leaders afford to ignore the short term, or even to privilege a long-term perspective over a short-term one? By 'zooming-out' and looking at the wider system we can see how the short term and the long term inter-connect – not as an opposing dualism but as a duality where each co-exists alongside the other, much as the concepts of *yin* and *yang* in Chinese philosophy. The reality is that leaders must manage for the short term *and* the long term, simultaneously; and the same is true of cost and quality, speed and accuracy and many other apparent dualities that leaders face in their working life.

It is worth noting, too, that every system is part of a larger system. Ken Wilber (1982) refers to this as the 'holographic paradigm' where reality comprises of 'holons' (something that is simultaneously a whole and a part), organised within a nested hierarchy. Hence, an individual may be part of a group, which is part of an organisation, which is part of a town, which is part of a region, which is part of a country, and so on. From this perspective each view of reality is both whole and yet also less than whole, because outside it there is another larger whole of which it is only a part, and beyond that is another.

The complex and contested landscape of leadership and management in a globalised society renders paradox an inescapable feature of organisational life. As Professor Ralph Stacey (2012) suggests: 'there is a major contradiction between the organisational reality of uncertainty and the beliefs that we have about the capacity of executives to know what is going on and be in control.'

In a literature review for the Virtual Staff College Ghate *et al.* (2013) identified an interesting coming together of theory and practice under the label of 'systems leadership', which is being advocated by organisations such as the Kings Fund in response to the challenges of integration and austerity within UK health and social care. Systems leadership is described as 'a collective form of leadership' concerned with 'the concerted effort of many people working together at different places in the system and at different levels' that 'crosses boundaries, both physical and virtual, existing simultaneously in multiple dimensions' (Ghate *et al.*, 2013, p. 6).

Whilst systems leadership tends to focus on the public sector context the importance of 'boundary spanning leadership' in private sector organisations is highlighted in research by the Center for Creative Leadership, which found that:

> 86% of senior executives believe it is 'extremely important' for them to work effectively across boundaries in their current leadership role. Yet, only 7% of these executives believe they are currently 'very effective' at doing so. That's a 79% gap!
>
> *(Yip* et al.*, 2009, p. 4)*

Effective leadership across boundaries requires leadership to be enacted through inter-personal influence rather than formal authority. In this case, issues of social identity come to the fore (as discussed in Chapter 7) and impact upon the extent to which a 'leader' is perceived as trustworthy, legitimate and/or competent by potential followers.

Finding a way forward in a uncertain world

The subtitle to this book, and underlying premise on which it is based, is that we need to rethink traditional concepts of leadership for an uncertain world. As discussed in Chapter 3, the acronym VUCA (volatile, uncertain, complex and ambiguous) is being used increasingly to describe the political, social, environmental and organisational context in which leaders are being asked to lead (Johansen, 2009).[4] Institutions such as the Forum for the Future and the Millennium Project, that forecast future trends, point to major global challenges over the coming decades including environmental degradation and rising social inequality (see, for example, Glenn *et al.*, 2014), that will have major impacts on the need for leadership.

In 'circumstances of high uncertainty and ideological and political contestation', Flinn and Mowles (2014, p. 19) suggest, 'leadership development involves encouraging radical doubt, enquiry and reflexivity' amongst leaders and organisations. Radical doubt, however, is the last thing that most organisations actively encourage, even if it may be exactly what is needed in order to break out of fixed and ineffective ways of leading and managing.[5]

In this book we suggest that recognising and engaging with the inherent paradoxes of leadership can be a powerful way of beginning to let go of our illusions of certainty and control and may forge the way for the development of more nuanced and 'wise' ways of leading. In so doing, we engage with the underlying philosophical questions of leadership, rather than simply seeing it as a technical problem to be solved. As Grint (2007) suggests:

> Leadership is not just a technical problem requiring greater *skills* – what Aristotle referred to as *techné* – if it was we would presumably have found the appropriate training system some time ago. Nor is it just a problem of understanding, requiring greater *knowledge*, what Aristotle called *episteme*; again, if it was we should be less at its mercy today than we were 100 years ago, but it seems we are not. In addition, it may also require greater *wisdom* – Aristotle's *phronesis* – through which leaders develop the wisdom to see what the good might be in the particular situation and then enact the processes that generate the good. In other words, it requires a form of action that focuses directly on fixing *the problem* itself, not a form of re-education or reskilling that fixes *the people*.
>
> *(p. 242, original emphasis)*

We propose the concept of leadership paradoxes, not as a map, but as a compass that can help steer us forward in uncertain times and to reconnect us with fundamental questions about purpose and possibility.

> The ultimate power of paradox derives from its liberating potential. While it draws attention to what might be seen as a negative message that no 'solution' is sustainable, its optimistic side is energizing: new opportunities of a surprising kind are possible when paradox is accepted and its potential realized.
>
> *(Storey and Salaman, 2009, p. 241)*

Questions for reflection and discussion

1. In this chapter we have highlighted some of the key themes raised throughout this book. To what extent do you agree with our summary? What have we missed that struck you as important? What are the key points or insights for you and your own professional practice and development as a leader?
2. Whilst we do not provide a definitive definition of leadership we recognise that definitions and descriptions can be useful in capturing and communicating key ideas. Take some time to review leadership definitions and quotes online and identify three complementary accounts that resonate with your own views and experience. If you are working in a group, share your thoughts with others and take time to reflect on what your choice of quotes and definitions says about your own values and assumptions.
3. In this chapter we distinguish between tame, wicked and critical problems. Take a few minutes to think about the main challenges you face at work (or case study organisation of your choice). Can you identify problems that clearly fall into any of these three categories? What leadership response(s) would each call for?
4. Leading across boundaries requires us to be aware of the social identities that are important to us, and those we seek to lead. On a sheet of paper list as many of the social identities that relate to you as possible and do the same for those you seek to lead. Do you notice any significant areas of mismatch? What could be done to help improve the fit between what your followers are looking for and what you represent?
5. Leadership requires us to create a path forward in an uncertain and unknowable world. Take time to draw up an action plan detailing what practical steps you could take to help create the future you hope to achieve for yourself and/or your organisation. What support would you need to get there and how can you access this?

Notes

1 Brynjolfsson and McAfee (2012) cite evidence to indicate that Moore's Law – that predicted a doubling of the processing power of computers every 12 months – is still true 50 years after it was first mooted, although the period of doubling is now recognised as around 18 months.

2 The phrase 'the map is not the territory', popularised by Alfred Korzybski, is a useful reminder that our theories and frameworks of leadership are mere representations – not 'leadership' itself. Indeed we are each likely to have multiple 'maps' of leadership, for use in different situations and for different purposes.
3 For more on the distinction between different types of system see Snowden and Boone (2007).
4 As an aside, it seems to us that VUCA also is a perfect term for describing paradoxes, which are often volatile, frequently uncertain, usually complex and almost always ambiguous. If one can lead through conditions of paradox, surely one can also lead in a VUCA environment.
5 The emerging field of 'Critical Leadership Studies' actively promotes the use of approaches that engage critically with underlying assumptions and issues of power (Collinson, 2011; Alvesson and Spicer, 2012).

Recommended reading

Bolden, R., Hawkins, B., Gosling, J. and Taylor, S. (2011) *Exploring Leadership: Individual, Organizational and Societal Perspectives*. Oxford: Oxford University Press.
Carroll, B., Ford, J. and Taylor, S. (2015) *Leadership: Contemporary Critical Perspectives*. London: Sage.
Grint, K. (2007) Learning to lead: can Aristotle help us find the road to wisdom? *Leadership*, 3(2), 231–246.
Handy, C. (1994) *The Age of Paradox*. Boston, MA: Harvard Business School Press.
Mowles, C. (2015) *Managing in Uncertainty: Complexity and the Paradoxes of Everyday Organizational Life*. London: Routledge.
Sinclair, A. (2007) *Leadership for the Disillusioned: Moving Beyond Myths and Heroes to Leading that Liberates*. Crows Nest, NSW: Allen & Unwin.

References

Alvesson, M. and Spicer, A. (2012) Critical leadership studies: the case for critical performativity, *Human Relations*, 65(3), 367–390.
Barton, D. (2011) Capitalism for the long term, *Harvard Business Review*, 89(3), 84–91.
Bennis, W. (2007) The challenges of leadership in the modern world: an introduction to the special issue, *American Psychologist*, 62(1), 2–5.
Bolden, R. (2011) Distributed leadership in organizations: a review of theory and research, *International Journal of Management Reviews*, 13(3), 251–269.
Bolden, R. and Gosling, J. (2006) Leadership competencies: time to change the tune? *Leadership*, 2(2), 147–163.
Bolden, R., Wood, M. and Gosling, J. (2006) Is the NHS Leadership Qualities Framework missing the wood for the trees? in A. Casebeer, A. Harrison and A.L. Mark (eds), *Innovations in Health Care: A Reality Check* (pp. 17–29). New York, NY: Palgrave Macmillan.

Brynjolfsson, E. and McAfee, A. (2012) Winning the race with ever smarter machines, *MIT Sloan Management Review*, 53(2), 53–60.

Ciulla, J. (2002) Trust and the future of leadership', in N.E. Bowie (ed.), *The Blackwell Guide to Business Ethics* (pp. 334–351). Oxford: Blackwell.

Ciulla, J. (2006) What we learned along the way: a commentary, in G.R. Goethals and G.L.J. Sorenson (eds), *The Quest for a General Theory of Leadership* (pp. 221–233). Cheltenham: Edward Elgar.

Collinson, D. (2011) Critical leadership studies, in A. Bryman, D. Collinson, K. Grint, B. Jackson and M. Uhl-Bien (eds), *The Sage Handbook of Leadership* (pp. 179–192). London: Sage.

Drath, W.H., McCauley, C.D., Palus, C.J., Van Velsor, E., O'Connor, P.M.G. and McGuire, J.B. (2008) Direction, alignment, commitment: toward a more integrative ontology of leadership, *The Leadership Quarterly*, 19(6), 635–653.

Fletcher, J. (2002) The greatly exaggerated demise of heroic leadership: gender, power, and the myth of the female advantage, *CGO Insights*, 13, 1–4.

Flinn, K. and Mowles, C. (2014) A complexity approach to leadership development: developing practical judgement. LFHE Stimulus Paper, London: Leadership Foundation for Higher Education.

Ghate, D., Lewis, J. and Welbourn, D. (2013) Systems leadership: exceptional leadership for exceptional times. Synthesis report. Nottingham: Virtual Staff College.

Gittings, R. (1968) *John Keats*. London: Heinemann.

Glenn, J.C., Gordon, T.J. and Florescu, E. (2014) *The Millennium Project: 2013–14 State of the Future: Executive Summary*. Washington, DC: The Millennium Project.

Grint, K. (2005a) *Leadership: Limits and Possibilities*. Basingstoke: Palgrave Macmillan.

Grint, K. (2005b) Problems, problems, problems: the social construction of 'leadership', *Human Relations*, 58(11), 1467–1494.

Grint, K. (2007) Learning to lead: can Aristotle help us find the road to wisdom? *Leadership*, 3(2), 231–246.

Grint, K. (2008) Wicked problems and clumsy solutions: the role of leadership, *Clinical Leader*, 1(2), 54–68.

Handy, C. (1994) *The Age of Paradox*. Boston, MA: Harvard Business School Press.

Heifetz, R.A., Grashow, A. and Linsky, M. (2009) *The Practice of Adaptive Leadership: Tools and Tactics for Changing Your Organization and the World*. Boston, MA: Harvard Business Review Press.

Johansen, B. (2009) *Leaders Make the Future*. San Francisco: Berrett-Koehler.

Mabey, C. and Mayrhofer, W. (eds) (2015) *Developing Leadership: Questions Business Schools Don't Ask*. London: Sage.

Pye, A. (2005) Leadership and organizing: sensemaking in action, *Leadership*, 1(1), 31–50.

Rittell, H. and Webber, M. (1973) Dilemmas in a general theory of planning, *Policy Sciences*, 4, 155–169.

Salaman, G. (2004) Competences of managers, competences of leaders, in J. Storey (ed.), *Leadership in Organizations: Current Issues and Key Trends* (pp. 58–78). London: Routledge.

Simpson, P., French, R. and Harvey, C. (2002) Leadership and negative capability, *Human Relations*, 55(10), 1209–1226.

Sinclair, A. (2007) *Leadership for the Disillusioned: Moving Beyond Myths and Heroes to Leading that Liberates*. Crows Nest, NSW: Allen & Unwin.

Smircich, L. and Morgan, G. (1982) Leadership: the management of meaning, *Journal of Applied Behavioural Science*, 18(3), 257–273.

Snowden, D. and Boone, M.E. (2007) A leader's framework for decision-making, *Harvard Business Review*, November, 69–76.

Stacey, R. (2012) *Tools and Techniques of Leadership and Management: Meeting the Challenge of Complexity*. London: Routledge.

Storey, J. and Salaman, G. (2009) *Managerial Dilemmas: Exploiting Paradox for Strategic Leadership*. Chichester: John Wiley and Sons.

Weick, K. (2012) Organized sensemaking: a commentary on processes of interpretive work, *Human Relations*, 65(1), 141–153.

Wilber, K. (1982) *The Holographic Paradigm and Other Paradoxes: Exploring the Leading Edge of Science*. Boston, MA: Shambhala.

Yip, J., Ernst, C. and Campbell, M. (2009) *Boundary Spanning Leadership: Mission Critical Perspectives from the Executive Suite*. Centre for Creative Leadership.

INDEX